CANDLES &
CONIFERS

Also by Ruth Burgess:

A Book of Blessings
At Ground Level (out of print)
Eggs and Ashes (with Chris Polhill)
Friends and Enemies
Hear My Cry
Hay & Stardust
Praying for the Dawn (with Kathy Galloway)

CANDLES &
CONIFERS

Resources for All Saints' and Advent

Ruth Burgess

WILD GOOSE PUBLICATIONS

First published 2005 by

Wild Goose Publications, 4th Floor, Savoy House, 140 Sauchiehall St, Glasgow G2 3DH, UK.
Wild Goose Publications is the publishing division of the Iona Community.
Scottish Charity No. SCO03794. Limited Company Reg. No. SCO96243.
www.ionabooks.com

ISBN 1 901557 96 0

Cover painting and internal illustration © Scott Riley

**The publishers gratefully acknowledge the support of the Drummond Trust,
3 Pitt Terrace, Stirling FK8 2EY in producing this book.**

A catalogue record for this book is available from the British Library.

Overseas distribution:
Australia: Willow Connection Pty Ltd, Unit 4A, 3-9 Kenneth Road, Manly Vale, NSW 2093
New Zealand: Pleroma, Higginson Street, Otane 4170, Central Hawkes Bay
Canada: Bayard Distribution, 49 Front Street East, Toronto, Ontario M5E 1B3

Permission to reproduce any part of this work in Australia or New Zealand should be sought
from Willow Connection.

Printed by Bell & Bain, Thornliebank, Glasgow

GENERAL CONTENTS

CONTENTS IN DETAIL

Key to symbols	
✟	Prayer
⭕	Reading
⁘	Biblical reflection
♬	Liturgy
(((◯)))	Responses
♫	Song
✍	Story
📖	Sermon
🎭	Drama

	Key to symbols
✝	Prayer
🎵	Reading
✛	Biblical reflection
🎬	Liturgy
(((○)))	Responses
♫	Song
🎭	Story
📖	Sermon
🎭	Drama

Journeying through Advent   177

Prophets   193

Enter the angels   201

Key to symbols	
✟	Prayer
𝄞	Reading
✤	Biblical reflection
𝄞	Liturgy
((◉))	Responses
♫	Song
🖎	Story
📖	Sermon
🎭	Drama

For Jenny
Grower of all things green, red and golden

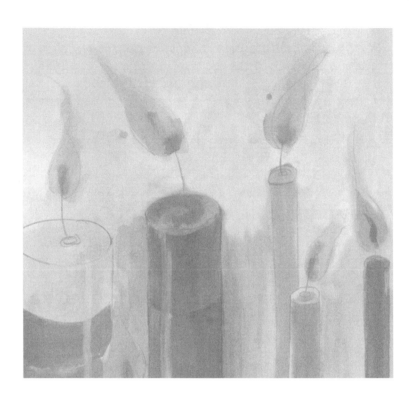

INTRODUCTION

Candles & Conifers is a resource book for November and December. It covers the period from All Saints' Day to Christmas Eve. It is a companion volume to *Hay & Stardust* (Wild Goose Publications), which covers the period from Christmas Day to Candlemas.

Whilst a number of complete liturgies are included, most of the material in this book consists of the stuff that liturgies are made of – stories, prayers, ceremonies, songs, responses, poems and biblical reflections.

The material is arranged chronologically, with sections relating to particular days and to general Advent themes. I have, in the contents pages, classified the material into types, for ease of reference.

My grateful thanks to all the contributors for the wealth and range of material that I have been privileged to edit. One book swiftly turned into two! Opening my mail has been a pleasure and a delight.

Thanks are also due to the Wild Goose Publications team, to Jane Darroch-Riley, Alex O'Neill, Tri Boi Ta and Sandra Kramer for their professionalism, encouragement and support; and to Neil Paynter, whose attention to detail is becoming legendary; I am hugely and gratefully in debt.

May you light your candles with hope and wonder.
May you live in justice and holy joy.

Ruth Burgess
Summer 2005

SAINTS AND SOULS

LIGHT A CANDLE

Voice 1:   Light a candle
Voice 2:   Light a candle for saints and sinners
Voice 3:   Light a candle with hope

A candle may be lit

Voice 1:   Light a candle
Voice 2:   Light a candle for all of creation
Voice 3:   Light a candle with joy

A candle may be lit

Voice 1:   Light a candle
Voice 2:   Light a candle for hope and wonder
Voice 3:   Light a candle with love

A candle may be lit

Ruth Burgess

BEINN A' CHOCHUILL*

All Saints' tide,
and bridal snow
smoothes over the rocks and wrinkles
of the ancient face.
It seems almost profane,
step by thrusting step,
to indent a track across.
But onward, upward,
it is clear, we are not the first:
someone has been before –
yesterday at a guess –
and where their feet have been,
compacted snow stands
like stepping stones. The wind
has blown away all that is powder,
dry, like sand. Only the steps remain,
and tell us it can be done.

Alan Horner   **A Munro in Scotland*

I'M NOT GOING TO SING

'I'm not going to sing,' he said,
and he spent the next thirty minutes
kicking at hassocks,
dropping his 10p (which, naturally,
never made it to the collection plate)
and retrieving it from under the pew.
Surprisingly (to my mind) he was silent
during the prayers –
and never forgot the Amen.
Then – he was the one the 'prayer man'
(as he called him) chose to wear
a cardboard halo.
Saint Michael – falling up the aisle.
Saint Michael – with a wicked grin
and six years
of laughter in him –
who refused to give back his halo
to the prayer man,
and wore it proudly home.
Blessed be God.
Blessed be God in his angels
and in all his saints.

Ruth Burgess

UNLIKELY SAINTS

The children sat on the floor in the story-area, but one wee boy stayed on the other side of the room. The teacher more or less dragged him over, and settled for him sitting on a chair facing the other way. It was my first time in that class. I started the story (Luke 19:1–10) and made it quite dramatic, adding in some possible background to Zacchaeus's life; talking about someone who'd always been small – born small, the smallest at school, getting bullied because of it – deciding he didn't need friends, being quite bright and doing well in his schoolwork, getting a good job that gave him lots of money, not caring whether people liked him or not. When Jesus came to town he wanted to check him out – he'd heard about some miracles, a blind man being cured; who was this guy?

As I was telling the story, I became aware of the boy on the edge of the group sneaking a look at me over his shoulder, and then, very slowly, swivelling round in his chair. He laughed along with the others when I described Zacchaeus almost falling out of the tree at the shock of Jesus speaking to him. I've never seen a child so intent, and it was hard to keep looking at the whole class. Afterwards I gave out a word search and he was the first one to finish it, rushing over to ask if he could draw a picture on the back of 'the wee man in the tree'. The teacher was pretty pleased, and I floated out of the class allowing myself a little pat on the back but mainly bowled over by the power of that story.

We may like to see ourselves in Zacchaeus – identifying with his willingness to change, admiring his commitment to be generous, feeling the warm glow of being forgiven and welcomed. But, once we've experienced all that, perhaps we should recognise in ourselves the tendency to be like the muttering crowd. The crowd whose response to hearing Jesus invite himself to Zacchaeus's house was puzzlement, irritation, even disgust. 'He's gone to be the guest of a sinner.' *Why didn't he come to my house? Or at least go with someone who's done some good in the community.*

Jesus called unlikely people to be saints and we often need to look for them in improbable places.

Liz Gibson

ST FRANCES OF ROME*

Saints are traditionally virgins (preferably martyrs)
but St Frances bucked the trend,
being both wife and mother
and finding time for good works too.
Was she a miracle worker, I wonder?
Or did she have an au pair?

Frances Copsey

St Frances (1338–1440) is known for her charity to the poor. Her feast day is March 9th.

RESPONSES FOR ALL SAINTS' DAY

Lectionary readings: Rev 7:2–4,9–14; Ps 24; 1 Jn 3:1–3; Mt 5:1–12

Opening responses

Seeking your wisdom
WE SEEK YOUR FACE

Seeking your integrity
WE SEEK YOUR FACE

Seeking your forgiveness
WE SEEK YOUR FACE

Seeking your strength
WE SEEK YOUR FACE

Seeking your beauty
WE SEEK YOUR FACE

Closing responses

Summoned to holiness
Roused to justice
WE ARE CALLED TO LIVE IN LOVE

Granted forgiveness
Blessed with mercy
WE ARE CALLED TO LIVE IN HOPE

Beckoned by saints
Encouraged by angels
WE ARE CALLED TO LIVE IN JOY

Ruth Burgess

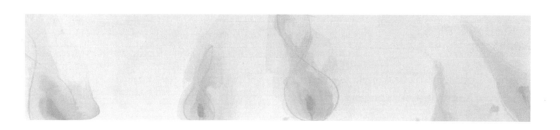

BIDDING PRAYERS FOR ALL SAINTS' DAY

God of warmth and welcome,
we come into your presence with wonder and praise;
caught up with the saints and the angels,
we bring you ourselves and our prayers:

We pray for all who hunger and thirst for what is right, for those who are prepared to stand up for justice and defend unpopular causes.

God, in your mercy,
HEAR OUR PRAYER

We give you thanks for the saints of Northumbria: for the vision of Cuthbert and the wisdom of Hilda, for the patience and trust of Aidan, for the poetry of Caedmon and the faithfulness of Bede. We thank you for their humanity, for their mistakes and successes, for their love for you.*

We pray for peacemakers; for peacemakers who live and work in places of conflict, for peacemakers who live in our own communities and homes.

God, in your mercy,
HEAR OUR PRAYER

We pray for those known to us who are ill, or in trouble, or in any kind of need.

God, in your mercy,
HEAR OUR PRAYER

We pray for those who have died, for those who, with the saints, are safe and joyful in God's keeping. Tell them we love them. Tell them we miss them.

God, in your mercy,
HEAR OUR PRAYER

We pray for ourselves ... called to be just and gentle ... for our hopes, our needs, our dreams.

God, in your mercy,
HEAR OUR PRAYER

Pilgrim God, lead us homewards.
May your saints encourage us,

your angels guard us,
and your little ones dance with us along the way.

Ruth Burgess

Include saints from your own area

A PRAYER FOR ALL SAINTS' DAY

Holy and merciful God,
write the values of the beatitudes
into our hearts and lives;
and help us,
with all your saints and angels,
to seek your face
and happily walk in your ways. Amen

Ruth Burgess

REMEMBER

Remember, remember where you are.
Remember, remember to tell us.
Remember, remember that you will be with me.

I remember when you were alive,
I remember when we played.
I remember when we would skateboard,
I remember when we played sticky in the mud.

I shall always remember us going to Boyne Park.

I shall always remember the sadness.

You made me laugh and laugh and laugh.

Debra Mullaly

Written at age 13, remembering her sister who was lost in a fatal road accident.

PRAYER OF ADORATION

(based on Isaiah 6:1–8)

O God who dwells in highest heaven,
yet stoops to touch my life,
I worship and adore you;
my voice mingles with the angels'
as I cry aloud:
'Holy, holy, holy are you, Lord of Hosts;
the whole earth is full of your glory.'

I am not worthy to touch the hem of your garment,
yet you call upon *me* to work for you here on earth.

You send your angels to me
and their healing touch blots out my sin.

I am overwhelmed by your glory;
I kneel in reverence and awe.

You ask me to stand up and go forth in your name.

O mighty, radiant, shattering God,
trembling, yet trusting, I reply:
'Here I am; send me.'

Irene Barratt

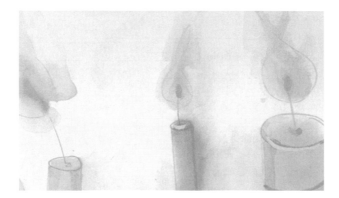

INDEPENDENCE

Independence is an illusion.
All that we have, all that we are,
comes to us from others.
We did not invent the technology of the wheel,
the comfort of a hot meal,
or even a toasted sandwich.

Why is it so hard to be dependent then
if age or illness makes us so?
I struggle against it,
blame my ego or my ignorance;
but if helplessness is my natural state should I
embrace it?
See it as a gift, a mark of shared humanity?
God knows.

Frances Copsey

AS A NET

Help us to realise that we are part of each other,
part of the whole world,
intertwined as a net.

Broaden our thinking,
stretch our imagination;
make us aware
that, in both giving and taking,
we are part of the whole.

In our hands is the ability to destroy or to build up.
Help us to make our choices wisely. Amen

Jean Murdoch

THE SAINTS OF GOD

Words and music: Ian M Fraser

The saints of God are down our street
and round God's throne of light.
There's some with formidable minds
and some in crafts delight;
together in God's family
their different gifts unite.

They serve at check-outs, empty bins,
they teach and make and mend;
they feed the hungry back from school,
the victimised defend;
to voiceless folk they lend an ear
and immigrants befriend.

Their efforts gain no accolades,
they simply earn that grace
which heals this world of many sores,
renews its battered face –
through such, who live and love and care
in their own time and place.

When death comes knocking at their door
they'll look at Christ askance –
how could such ordinary lives
his Kingdom ends advance?
But Christ will say, 'It's party time –
come, friends, and join my dance.'

Ian M Fraser

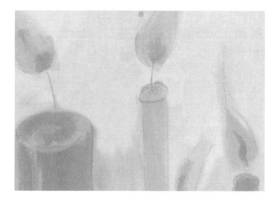

A LITANY FOR ALL SAINTS'

FOR THOSE WHO LIT OUR LIVES WITH JOY,
FOR THOSE WHO HAVE TOUCHED US WITH TENDERNESS,
FOR THOSE WHOSE LOSS FILLS US WITH LONGING,
WE GIVE THANKS IN GLAD REMEMBRANCE.

We celebrate those who have loved us for ourselves,
looking with acceptance on all that we are,
and cherishing us without condition or constraint.
HOLY GOD, WITHIN AND AMONGST US,
WE GIVE THANKS IN GLAD REMEMBRANCE.

We celebrate those who have stood alongside us,
holding us in the depths of elation or despair
where words of joy or rescue fall silent.
HOLY GOD, WITHIN AND AMONGST US,
WE GIVE THANKS IN GLAD REMEMBRANCE.

We celebrate those who would not let us stand still,
edging us gently into the open space
of new understanding and delighted exploration.
HOLY GOD, WITHIN AND AMONGST US,
WE GIVE THANKS IN GLAD REMEMBRANCE.

We celebrate those who have challenged us to grow,
perceiving all that we have it in us to become
and daring us to dream beyond our imagining.
HOLY GOD, WITHIN AND AMONGST US,
WE GIVE THANKS IN GLAD REMEMBRANCE

We celebrate those who have travelled before us,
showing us in their persistent courage and tenderness
how to live in love, and die in faith and hope.
HOLY GOD, WITHIN AND AMONGST US,
WE GIVE THANKS IN GLAD REMEMBRANCE.

FOR THOSE WHO LIT OUR LIVES WITH JOY,
FOR THOSE WHO HAVE TOUCHED US WITH TENDERNESS,
FOR THOSE WHOSE LOSS FILLS US WITH LONGING,
WE GIVE THANKS IN GLAD REMEMBRANCE.

Jan Berry

FROM A SERVICE OF REMEMBRANCE AND TRAVELLING ON

Opening prayer

I am the resurrection and the life, says the Lord; those who believe in me shall live, even though they die, and no one who lives and trusts in me shall ever truly die. (John 11:25,26)

God of all life and of what comes beyond the life we know,
we come to you tonight in our need.
We come in our brokenness.
We come to you with our gratitude.
We come with loose ends that we have not been able to tie up.

We may not know why it is that we have come
or why you have led us here,
but we know that you have promised never to turn us away.

Prayer

God of all time, we say that time is a healer,
and yet healing does not happen without our permission.
If we come tonight with bitterness,
persuade us with your sweetness.
If we come tonight still with anger,
pacify us with your patience
If we come with pain,
soothe us with your tenderness.
If we come numb with shock,
calm us with your hand placed on our shoulders.
If we come in despair,
give us hope.

Invitation to light candles

Before the service, people are asked to give in names of people they want to be remembered. These names are read out during the lighting of the candles.

Leader: Light a light for those you want to remember.
            Light a light for hope.
            Light a light as a prayer beyond words.

Light a candle for those you need, in whatever way, to let go.
Take your time.
We have time enough tonight.

But first, let us pray ...
God of all life,
life here and now,
life beyond death;
God of many names,
reaching out through beliefs and traditions
and sometimes despite these things;
God reaching out with a hand to hold
and an ear to listen,
let your Spirit move amongst us,
let burdens be lifted,
let hearts be lightened.
May your suffering people find peace
and may those who mourn
know they are blessed in you.

People come forward to light candles. While candles are being lit and names are being read out, the chant God to Enfold You might be sung (John L. Bell & Graham Maule, Iona Abbey Music Book or Love & Anger, Wild Goose Publications).

Closing blessing

May God bless us
and heal us
and hold us in love,
today
tonight
and for evermore.
Amen

David Coleman

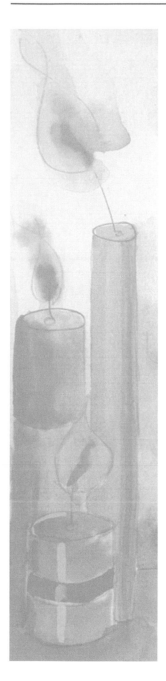

BORN ANEW

May Christ's being born
anew in our hearts,
bring light, healing and wholeness
to us and all our loved ones
in this world and in heaven.

And the saints shall tread
the pilgrim roads before us,
behind us,
between us,
surrounding us,
with the unbounded love
of God our Creator.

Yvonne Morland

THE MEMORY OF BEAUTY

The memory of beauty
is not erased by death.
God makes a blossom of it
in our wounded hearts,
and In the rich soil
of the lonely watches
of the night.

Yvonne Morland

BRIGHT GOD OF HEALING, SET US FREE

A women's winter liturgy with fireworks - originally written for November 5th/Guy Fawkes Night

Setting: Outdoors!

Opening prayer

God of light and beauty,
inspire our prayers;
put a bright halo of healing and glory
around us and around those we name tonight.
We ask our prayers in the fire and energy of the Holy Spirit,
and in the name of Jesus, the Light of the world. AMEN

We will light a Catherine wheel, which is a firework named after an instrument of torture used in the persecution of early Christian martyrs.

By lighting the Catherine wheel, we remember women tortured and persecuted throughout the ages.

The Catherine wheel is lit.

We remember the early Christian martyrs: Catherine, Agnes, Felicity, Perpetua, Agatha, Cecilia and Lucy …

We remember those women who were executed and imprisoned for their faith: Margaret Clitheroe, Margaret Ward, Anne Line, Margaret Pole, Rebecca Collingwood, Dorothy Vavasur, Ursula Taylor, Jane Corby, Dorothy Lawson …

We celebrate their courage, their generosity, their faithfulness.

We remember those wise women and healers who were burned as witches: Alice Nutter, Jane Demdike, Isobel Taylor, Mother Lakeland, Annabelle Stuart …

We celebrate their wisdom and skill.

We remember women raped and killed by enemy soldiers in many countries …

We honour them and share their pain.

We remember female children killed before and after birth because of their gender …

We suffer, for they are our loss.

We remember women lost to the world because of disease, malnutrition and discrimination …

We weep for them.

Here please feel free to name other women you wish to celebrate and remember …

Reading

You do not need to be afraid of dying in pain for I will be with you and your mind will be fixed on me … I will take your soul into my own hands which were nailed to the cross and offer it to my Father with incense and music, and you will see him. I shall take you by the hand and we will dance for joy in heaven with all the saints and angels who will rejoice at your coming.

Margery Kempe

Litany

From pain and weariness,
BRIGHT GOD OF HEALING, SET US FREE

From heavy burdens,
BRIGHT GOD OF HEALING, SET US FREE

From pride and bitterness,
BRIGHT GOD OF HEALING, SET US FREE

From past regret,
BRIGHT GOD OF HEALING, SET US FREE

From painful memories,
BRIGHT GOD OF HEALING, SET US FREE

From anxiety about the future,
BRIGHT GOD OF HEALING, SET US FREE

From deep despair,
BRIGHT GOD OF HEALING, SET US FREE

From guilt and terror,
BRIGHT GOD OF HEALING, SET US FREE

Reading

Our faith is a light, the kindly gift of that endless day which is our Father, God. By this light, our Mother Christ, and our good Lord the Holy Spirit lead us into this fleeting life. When the time of trial has passed, suddenly our eyes shall be opened and in the brightness of light we shall see fully. This light is God our maker, and the Holy Spirit in Christ Jesus our Saviour.

Julian of Norwich

Creed

WE BELIEVE IN GOD,
WHO BROUGHT FORTH LIGHT FROM CHAOS AND DARKNESS.
WE BELIEVE IN JESUS,
WHO FACED THE DARKNESS OF THE GRAVE
AND ROSE FROM DEATH TO LIFE AND GLORY.
WE BELIEVE IN THE HOLY SPIRIT,
WHO WALKS WITH US IN DARKNESS AND LIGHT.
WE BELIEVE THAT WE ARE SURROUNDED ALWAYS
BY A GREAT COMPANY OF SAINTS AND ANGELS.
WE BELIEVE THAT WE ARE CALLED TO SHARE AND PROCLAIM
THE JUSTICE AND WONDER OF GOD.
AMEN

Lighting the rockets

We light rockets to symbolise the glory of the saints in heaven and the power of the Holy Spirit lighting up our lives.

The rockets are lit in celebration.

Song: Pentecost: Like fireworks in the night (see p.33)

Blessing

May God, the brightness of the universe, bless us.
May Jesus, the light of the world, disturb us.
May the Holy Spirit, energy of the cosmos, strengthen us.
May we be blessed with the power to speak and live the gospel all our days. AMEN

Mary McHugh and Patricia Stoat

PENTECOST

(Tune: Love unknown. 6.6.6.6. 4.4.4.4)

Like fireworks in the night
the Holy Spirit came;
disciples' fears took flight
when touched by fronds of flame:
    and suddenly the world was young
    as hope embraced a Saviour's claim.

For Jesus bade them dare
to venture, as they should;
his love taught them to share
their homes, possessions, food:
    the mind of Jesus gave them speech
    all tribes and peoples understood.

Thus God our spirits lifts
fresh daring to inspire;
as common folk get gifts
to change the world entire:
    the tongues of flame at Pentecost
    ran through the world like forest fire

Ian M Fraser

NOVEMBER

Fireworks gone to bed now.
And next time you see them
you'll be nearer four,
and will your eyes shine as brightly
as they did tonight,
and will sparklers and Roman candles
still make you wriggle with excitement
and fill your face with such infectious joy?
And Neil,
will a bowl of warm crisps
put in front of you – at your level
with no one saying no –
still bring the moment
when your hands touch
the fullness of all your dreams?

Ruth Burgess

GRANDFATHER, 1978

He is sitting in a high-backed chair watching fat wrestlers on TV
the screen thicker than a cartoon character's glasses
and he knows it is all make-believe but he makes believe that he does not

his shirt grimy-collared   fraying around the cuffs   his trousers
great clown-worthy trousers held tight in the jaws of braces
and a belt surely made from the whole side of a cow

the liver-spotted arms   the muscles made thin as his hair
that finger   the third on his left hand   knuckled short
as if a knife has been taken to it as vicious as the one he uses
to de-string sausages for tea

and the sigh   the sigh he gives   heavy and long as winter
when finally I gulp up the courage to ask how the finger was lost
and the words   the words he speaks to seal the sigh

the words I understand even as a child are place names
but sound like injuries

Mametz   Neuve Chappelle   Wipers and finally
Passchendaele   said as if his mouth is clotted with mud

Rachel Mann

60+

Sixty years on I listened.
Old now, they spoke of then.
Of stumbling over greening dead,
of hunger and confusion,
of seeing friends get shot,
of the camp where few survived,
and the dreams they had,
and the silence
of things they never told,
till now.

They were gentle men.
Enjoying the garden
and walks down the lane.
They fought to stop invasion,
because they must
for all our freedom.

And I said, 'Thank you.
Thank you for the life
your youth
gave me.'

Chris Polhill

EDDIE

(From a longer story about working in a nursing home)

Returning from my rounds, I discover Eddie's up. Oh, he's up all right – naked, streaking up and down the cold narrow hallways, chanting, 'Jumpsuit, jumpsuit!'

I quickly catch up and direct him into a washroom.

Eddie's mind works in ruts it's difficult to jolt it out of – onto a different track of thought, onto a different subject.

'Jumpsuit, I want my jumpsuit or somethin'.' Eddie speaks with a lilt, a poet's rhythm – Bob Dylan at sixty-five.

I corral him into a stall and, gently as possible, both rough hands on his broad shoulders, push him firmly down onto a cold toilet seat.

'Yes, Eddie, I know you want to get dressed' – again he tries to rise. I hold him down with just enough pressure to let him know who's boss; that's how I've been instructed to handle Eddie. 'We'll put your jumpsuit on in just a minute. And it's the green one, the one you like best, the one we didn't shrink. But, first, see if you can go, OK?'

As I talk I quickly pull a thick leather restraint across Eddie's lap. Now that he is sitting it should be a great deal easier to communicate with Eddie. In just a few minutes after sitting down, Eddie's mind usually settles, clears, and then one is able to have quite a good chat with him about, say, politics, baseball, Chinese cooking, philosophy, gardening … He continues straining against his tether, while stroking his fuzzy, sagging breasts with the calloused tips of his burnt fingers. (Eddie smokes a pipe and has a collection of over fifteen, one from every country he visited.) Occasionally he tweaks his cold, erect nipples.

'Come on, jumpsuit. Goddamn jumpsuit.'

'So, Eddie,' – I see the concentration and strain on his old but still somehow boyish face as he works the muscles in his swollen abdomen – 'how's your garden coming along, any results?' Eddie helps the groundsman, Hal – 'Hal's my pal, Hal's my pal' – and has his own little plot out back.

'Like to kill that goddamn groundhog. The cute little bugger's been eatin' up all my lovely lettuce. Can't crap or somethin'.' (I hate putting Eddie through this morning ritual but if I don't, later in the day we could have a mess on our hands, the head nurse cautioned me.) Most of the hospital garden's grown over now. Rumours are they're going to close this place. After the World War One vets have all passed on, someone was saying at caffeine break the other day.

'Ya, saw a rainbow in the garden yesterday, in the spray, after it rained. Just stared. It was so goddamn beautiful. You don't see that too often. Too much goddamn pollution … Ya, like to shoot that gopher – the cute little bugger's been eatin' up all my lovely lettuce. Can't crap.'

I ask Eddie what books he's been reading lately. He reads war literature mostly – fiction, non-fiction – and devours several thick books a week. Last Sunday he'd just finished an epic Russian novel about the First World War. 'Solzhenitsyn's a goddamn good writer,' he advised. I ask him again what he's been reading but he doesn't answer me. He seems far away.

Eddie was a tail gunner in the Second World War. Stationed in England, he did runs over Germany and won nine medals. One for landing a crippled plane after his pilot was shot – at 18! (At 18, I couldn't even drive a car.) After the war he lived in big cities, at Sally Ann missions mostly, and, in the summertime, alone at a dead friend's cottage up north (so I read in his file). Finally, because he moved around so much, the Veterans' Affairs stopped issuing him cheques. They found him in the fall of 1963, at the crumbling cottage. He'd stopped eating and 'looked like an inmate from a concentration camp'. The place was stinking, the report said, littered with his faeces. A hero, he had become as helpless as a trapped dog who had lost its master. His mind had lost its master, and began to roam wildly.

The toilet flushes. I turn from the sink where I'm assembling towels and a face cloth. Eddie fiddles with himself underneath; he begins flushing the toilet repeatedly, frantically rattling the handle. 'Can't crap. Can't crap or somethin'!' And I realise he isn't wiping himself but fingering himself. The toilet overflows. I unchain Eddie and pull him off the toilet and out of the stall. He stands there naked, and again reaches up inside himself for his waste matter, for the poison that won't come.

I hurriedly put an Attends on Eddie.

'Don't need a goddamn diaper!'

'I'm sorry Eddie.'

No matter how many times I do it, it feels wrong putting a baby blue diaper on a man. On a man who was a hero.

'I'm sorry.'

'Don't need a goddamn diaper.'

I wash Eddie's hands and face; tell him to step into his jumpsuit; comb his thin head of hair; tie his new white runners; then send him away to play outside in the garden.

'Be back by lunch time, Eddie,' I remind him, as he trots off with excitement.

Out in the dayroom, the men sit planted underneath the television, eating maple-flavoured oatmeal; they droop like cut flowers in stagnant water. I gaze tiredly out of the window and suddenly see Eddie – running across the lawn in his green jumpsuit. The summer sky is a deep, clear blue, and it looks like he wants to take off into it.

Neil Paynter

ALL HEAVEN WEEPS
(for Remembrance Sunday)

Music: Carol Dixon, based on a Scottish air

All heaven weeps
To see the earth
Abused and maimed by war and strife,
When people hate,
When people fight,
And rob each other of their life.

Chorus: Kyrie eleison, kyrie eleison.
Lord have mercy, God forgive us,
For we know not what we do.

When greed prevails
And, crushed by power,
The poor are trampled on for gain,
The heart of God
Is torn in two,
And Christ is crucified again.

Chorus: twice

Carol Dixon

ST MARTIN OF TOURS
(St Martin's Day, November 11th)

Words: Kathy Galloway. Music: John Barnard

introduction

descant v. 5 only

5. So re- joice ___ peo-ple in all pla - ces for the saints whose

com-pa - ny we share. Oh give voice ___ peo-ple of all ra - ces

molto rall. (last time only)

to the Spi - rit's hope and live it ev - ery - where.

'I am Christ's soldier and I cannot fight.'
For the God of peace, you put your sword away;
and with heart aching for a poor man's plight,
gave him half your cloak one bitter winter's day.
Was it so, Martin, did your vision lead you
to a hermit's cell and to a bishop's care?
Did you know, Martin, that your Lord would need you
to renew the common life of love and prayer?

Some were Christ's prophets, speaking truth to power,
in a world gone mad with bloodlust, hate and fear.
And a voice broke upon a Babel tower,
crying, 'Why speak peace, when there is no peace here!'
O be heard, brothers, in today's confusion,
that the claim of justice never be ignored;
may your word, sisters, reach through each illusion
till true dignity to all shall be restored.

Some were Christ's healers of the world's unmaking,
binding up the wounds of earth's unending strife.
They brought love's mending to the poor heart breaking,
bearing in themselves the promise of new life.
As you stood, sisters, with the dispossessed ones,
stand beside us too, who fear what we might lose;
yet we would, brothers, walk beside the blessed ones.
Christ is there, inviting us to hear good news.

Some were Christ's lovers, with a passion springing
from the mystery that would not let them go;
and as joy wells up and pours out in singing,
so God's grace expressed in them would overflow.
By your prayers, fathers, you stretch out and reach us
in our darkest moments, offering us new worth.
In our cares, mothers, you inform and teach us
that love's pain and labour herald love's new birth.

We are Christ's people and this is our story,
of the body broken that we might be free.
In his love risen, let us see the glory
in our imperfection, and what's yet to be.
So rejoice, people, in all times and places,
for the company of saints in which we share;
O give voice, people of all kinds and races,
to the Spirit's hope, and live it everywhere.

Kathy Galloway
Written for the Patronal Festival of St Martin-in-the-Fields Church, London

ANDREWTIDE

(Suggested tune: Angelus, or any other slow, reflective 8.8.8.8. tune)

The crowd had listened to your word,
With love their hearts and minds were fired;
The miracle of what they heard
Still kept them close, though hungry, tired.

As daylight left the crowded slope,
You saw their simple human need,
Sent Andrew and the rest in hope,
To find, to gather, and to feed.

The smallest gift a child could share,
Some bread, two fishes, simple food,
Broke in your hands to love and care,
To feed the hungry multitude.

Like Andrew, now we turn and seek;
Earth's hunger haunts us, stark and real;
We fear the gifts we find too weak
The world's distress to touch and heal.

Now send us, searching, for the gift
That hides in every human soul,
That in your hands sin's power can shift
And love can make creation whole.

Use us, your friends, to seek and trace
The gift that seems of smallest worth,
To shape the miracle of grace,
The love to feed a hungry earth.

Anna Briggs

THE DAY AFTER JOHN LENNON DIED

(John Lennon was shot and killed in New York City on December 8, 1980.)

The day after John Lennon died
my father made me
bacon and eggs and
toast and tea and
set up a TV table
in the den.

He met me at the bottom of the stairs.
'Did you hear?' he asked.

Then he told me the news.

'I turned on the television for you,
I thought you might want to –
They're re-playing his life,' he said,
and left me alone.

I sat on the edge of the couch
and stared
Good Morning Fucked up America.[1]

That night my father said he remembered hearing
when Glen Miller's plane crashed.

At school that day
I sat out gym class
(even though it was co-ed
and I lost points).

They were teaching us 'modern dance' that semester.

We sat up in the bleachers, [2]
the three of us,
(Joe, me and Mikehead)
and, while everyone
did the bump and the hustle –
'Do the hus-tle'–
we talked about *The White Album*.

Mrs Fern switched off all the lights suddenly;
everybody went: 'Wooooooo!'

The mirrored ball
(left over from last year's prom)
turned slowly from the rafters –
like an empty, glittery world.

'Sure you boys don't want to change your minds
and come and join in?'
she called
over Disco Duck.[3]
Everyone out on the gymnasium floor
had white spots –
like some disco disease.

The three of us talked
about what it must have been like
to hear *Sergeant Pepper's*
when it first came out.
Musta been incredible.
Joe said he knew a guy,
one of his big brother Frankie's friends,
who was driving along in his car
and had to pull over when it first came on the radio –
just had to fuckin' pull right over.
Man, imagine that.
'Imagine,' we all said together,
and bowed our heads.

'Sergeant Pepper's was mostly all Paul McCartney, you know,'
Peter Roach said, dumdeduming,
breaking the silence,
coming to sit down
with us.
'No way!'
'No fuckin' way, what are ya talkin' about?
And quit your spittin', ya pinhead.
I had a shower already this morning.'

'Look Roach, Mikehead should know, man.'

(Mikehead was a Beatles freak,
had rare German bootlegs,
every single
solo album – even all Ringo's)

On a sheet of loose leaf,
lifted carefully from Mikehead's duotang, 4
we composed a eulogy to have read
over the P.A.
after noon announcements:

May John Winston Lennon
sleep in Golden Slumbers
until The End

May we all
Come Together and
Carry That Weight

How we wish he were Only Sleeping

That evening
my parents had the next door neighbours over for dinner.
The Drummonds
Leonard and Eleanor.

Passing the murdered slab of
rare roast beef,
Mrs Drummond remarked,
'And all this business about John Lennon being shot,
when what they should be talking about
are those nuns in El Salvador who were massacred –
now *that* was terrible.'
'Who?' said my mother. 'Where?'
Juice puddled on the white china platter.
I threw down my serviette
and stomped upstairs to my bedroom,
to crank up All We Are Saying Is Give Peace a Chance
on my Panasonic stereo (with Bose speakers) you could hear pounding
through the thin, suburban floor.

In history class,
on the first anniversary
of the death
of John Lennon,
Mr Van Diemen quizzed,
'OK, now does anyone know

what happened on this date
in history?'

Joe's hand shot up before anyone's.
(Joe only ever put up his hand to go to the washroom,
to go and smoke a 'dove-tailed'[5] joint.)

Van Diemen's narrow, grey eyes searched the classroom,
everybody half-asleep
in the fluorescent drone,
and focused on my friend
finally.

'Lennon died,'
was all Joe said
and put down his hand.

Light glinted and swirled off Van Diemen's
burnished bald head as
he tisked
    and chuckled
and tisked
    and chuckled
'Joe, Joe, Joe, Joe, Joe ...'
– on the weekends Van Diemen golfed and crushed
fragile young egos at a militia barracks some place –
'Joe, Joe, Joe, Joe, Joe...'

'That's my name, don't wear it out,' answered Joe.

'Vladimir Ilyich *Lenin* died on the
twenty-first of January
in nineteen hundred and twenty-four.'
'No, John *Len-non*,'
Joe pronounced.

'Oh, him' –
Van Diemen shooed the Beatle's
memory and influence aside –
'he doesn't matter.'

'Don't worry about it, Joe,'

I whispered up the row.
'Van Diemen's a bullet head.'

I started humming
strains of
Working Class Hero
then Revolution
then Happy Christmas War is Over (if you want it)
a couple of people got it.
Van Diemen went on about the Cold War and
Richard Milhouse Nixon.
We never did find out
what else happened
on December 8th
in history.

Neil Paynter

1 Good Morning America is a TV programme.

2 Bleachers: stands, seats in a gymnasium

3 Disco Duck is a very bad disco song.

4 A duotang is a type of three-ringed binder.

5 Reference to the John Lennon song 'Happiness is a Warm Gun' from The Beatles' White Album

CHRIST THE KING

RESPONSES

Cycle A
Ez 34:11–12,15–17; Ps 23; 1Cor 15:20–26,28; Mt 25:31– 46

From mist and darkness
From restful waters
GOD GATHERS US

From health and sickness
From plenty and poverty
GOD GATHERS US

From highroads and byways
From fields and cities
GOD GATHERS US

To a feast, a banquet,
To life eternal
GOD GATHERS US SAFE HOME

> Christ the King
> King of justice
> WE BELONG TO YOU

> Christ the King
> King of glory
> WE BELONG TO YOU

> Christ the King
> King of integrity
> WE BELONG TO YOU

Cycle B
Dan 7:13,14; Ps 93; Rev 1:5–8; Jn 18:33–37

From all eternity
Bright and beautiful
GOD IS GOD

Alpha and Omega
Integrity and holiness
GOD IS GOD

Truth and vulnerability
Majesty and mystery
GOD IS GOD

　God was
　In the beginning
　BRINGING WONDER AND LIGHT

　God is
　In the present
　BRINGING TRUTH AND LOVE

　God will be
　In the future
　BRINGING HOPE AND TRUTH

　Or:

　Today and tomorrow
　In time and eternity
　YOUR KINGDOM COME

　In our world, in our streets
　In our homes and communities
　YOUR KINGDOM COME

　In our lives, in our loves
　In our hopes and our travelling
　YOUR KINGDOM COME

Cycle C
2 Sam 5:1–3; Ps 122; Col 1:11–20; Lk 23:35–43

Strength through vulnerability
Peace through pain
JESUS IS THE IMAGE OF THE UNSEEN GOD

Justice through questioning
Light through darkness
JESUS IS THE IMAGE OF THE UNSEEN GOD

Courage through truth
Love through reconciliation
JESUS IS THE IMAGE OF THE UNSEEN GOD

Or:

For Jews and gentiles
For friends and strangers
YOU PASSED THROUGH DARKNESS INTO LIGHT

For judges and criminals
For disciples and enemies
YOU PASSED THROUGH DARKNESS INTO LIGHT

For people like us
For each one of us
YOU PASSED THROUGH DARKNESS INTO LIGHT

    IN THE STRENGTH OF JESUS
    WE ARE POWERFUL
    Never give in to evil.

    IN THE PEACE OF JESUS
    WE ARE FORGIVEN
    Never give in to evil.

    IN THE LOVE OF JESUS
    WE ARE ENCIRCLED
    Never give in to evil.

Ruth Burgess

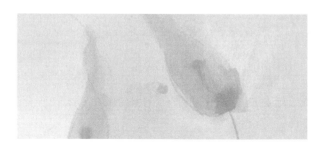

THE RETURN OF THE KING
A liturgy

Opening responses

Reader: In his days justice shall flourish,
            and peace, till the moon fails *(Psalm 72:7)*
ALL: IN HIS DAYS JUSTICE SHALL FLOURISH
         AND THE VOICES OF THOSE WHO ARE OPPRESSED WILL BE HEARD.
         THE POOR WILL RECEIVE ENOUGH ON WHICH TO LIVE,
         AND THE RICH WILL SHARE GLADLY
         THE ABUNDANCE THEY HAVE RECEIVED AT THE HAND OF GOD.

Reader: In his days justice shall flourish,
            and peace, till the moon fails.
ALL: THE WOLF WILL LIE DOWN WITH THE LAMB:
         THE FIERCE WILL GIVE WAY TO THE TAME,
         THE WEAK WILL PROTECT THE STRONG,
         THE POWERLESS WILL CONTAIN THE POWER OF THE MIGHTY.

Reader: In his days justice shall flourish,
            and peace, till the moon fades.
ALL: GOD WILL GIVE JUDGEMENT TO THE KING,
         TO THE ONE WHO COMES IN THE NAME OF THE LORD
         TO ESTABLISH PEACE AND JUSTICE
         WITH INTEGRITY AND WITH MERCY.

Scripture reading: Isaiah 11:1–10

Litany

Reader: Into places of conflict
ALL: MAY YOUR KINGDOM COME
Reader: Into the hearts of terrorists
ALL: MAY YOUR KINGDOM COME
Reader: Into the hearts of soldiers
ALL: MAY YOUR KINGDOM COME
Reader: Into the hearts of politicians
ALL: MAY YOUR KINGDOM COME
Reader: Into the hearts of those bereaved by war
ALL: MAY YOUR KINGDOM COME

Reader:	Into the hearts of those who are hungry
ALL:	MAY YOUR KINGDOM COME
Reader:	Into the hearts of those made homeless
ALL:	MAY YOUR KINGDOM COME
Reader:	Into the hearts of those who despair
ALL:	MAY YOUR KINGDOM COME
Reader:	Into the hearts of those who are ill
ALL:	MAY YOUR KINGDOM COME
Reader:	Into the hearts of those who have been abused
ALL:	MAY YOUR KINGDOM COME
Reader:	Into the hearts of those who are addicted
ALL:	MAY YOUR KINGDOM COME
Reader:	Into the hearts of those in debt
ALL:	MAY YOUR KINGDOM COME
Reader:	Into the hearts of those who are lonely
ALL:	MAY YOUR KINGDOM COME
Reader:	Into the hearts of those who are fearful
ALL:	MAY YOUR KINGDOM COME
Reader:	Into the hearts of those who are depressed
ALL:	MAY YOUR KINGDOM COME
Reader:	Into the hearts of those we name before you in the silence …
ALL:	MAY YOUR KINGDOM COME
Reader:	Into the heart of our world.
ALL:	MAY YOUR KINGDOM COME

Closing responses

Reader:	In his days justice shall flourish, and peace, till the moon fails.
ALL:	MERCY AND FAITHFULNESS SHALL MEET AND EMBRACE, AND THE GLORY OF GOD SHALL BE REVEALED IN BEAUTY, IN AWE AND IN WONDER.
Reader:	The King will establish his Kingdom.
ALL:	AND THE HAND OF THE KING, MIGHTY AND STRONG IN THE BATTLE WITH EVIL, SHALL BE THE HAND OF THE HEALER: OPENING THE EYES OF THOSE WHO ARE SLEEPING, RAISING PEOPLE TO THEIR FEET, AND REJOICING IN THEIR WELL-BEING.

Reader:　　And the Spirit of God shall be with him
ALL:　　AND UPON HIS PEOPLE.
　　　　　AND THEY SHALL KNOW THAT GOD HAS MADE HIS HOME WITH THEM.
　　　　　AND HE SHALL BE THEIR KING AND THEIR GOD
　　　　　AND THEY SHALL BE HIS PEOPLE:
　　　　　BLESSED BEYOND MEASURE,
　　　　　MADE RADIANT IN HIS LIGHT
　　　　　AND AT PEACE
　　　　　IN BODY,
　　　　　MIND
　　　　　AND SPIRIT.
　　　　　A PEOPLE MADE WHOLE
　　　　　BY THE RETURN OF THEIR KING.
　　　　　AMEN

From Wellspring

THE PEOPLE GOD CALLS BLESSED

If I'm reading it right*
the people God calls blessed
are the ones who
feed the hungry
welcome the stranger
befriend those in trouble
care for those in pain.

Not a word about
who or what they do or don't believe in,
only a description of how they live their lives.

So I ask a blessing, God,
on my friends
who cannot
or do not
believe in you.
A blessing that they are not expecting
yet one which they will recognise.
A blessing of joy, integrity and justice,
a blessing of love and life.

Ruth Burgess

* *Matthew 25:34–46*

PSALM 97

The Lord is King! Now all the earth be glad!
Rejoice you islands of the seas!
Clouds and deep darkness all around his throne;
He rules with right and equity.
Fire before him, lightning from above,
Hills become like wax before his face;
Heavens proclaim the righteousness of God;
His great glory shines in every place.

All who praise idols now are put to shame;
All gods bow down as he goes by;
Zion and Judah listen and rejoice;
He is the Lord of earth and sky:
He protects his people in his love,
Rescues them from out of the wicked's might;
In your God rejoice and give him thanks,
All you righteous live in joy and light.

Margaret Harvey

Psalm 97
Rhyfelgyrch Capten Morgan (Captain Morgan's March), traditional Welsh folk tune

WORLD AIDS DAY

December 1st

RESPONSES

Cycle A
Is 25:6–10; Ps 23; Mt 15:29–37

On your mountain
YOU WELCOME US

In your home
YOU WELCOME US

At your table
YOU WELCOME US

Our names are on your guest list
YOU WELCOME US WITH JOY.

> Give us new strength
> Guide our feet
> LEAD US HOME
>
> Take away our disgrace
> Wipe away our tears
> LEAD US HOME
>
> Protect us in darkness
> Save us from evil
> LEAD US HOME
>
> You are our shepherd
> You have what we need
> LEAD US HOME

Cycle B
Is 26:1–6; Ps 118; Mt 7:21,24–27

God our rock
YOUR LOVE IS ETERNAL

Jesus our cornerstone
YOUR LOVE IS ETERNAL

Holy Spirit our strength
YOUR LOVE IS ETERNAL

You are our goodness
You are our wisdom
YOU ARE OUR ROCK

You are our mercy
You are our justice
YOU ARE OUR ROCK

You are our love
You are our courage
YOU ARE OUR ROCK

You are our joy
You are our freedom
YOU ARE OUR ROCK

Cycle C
Is 2:1–5; Ps 122; Mt 8:5–11

Swords into ploughs
Spears into pruning hooks
WAR INTO PEACE

Seeds into fruit
Weeds into bonfires
HUNGER INTO FOOD

God will teach us what we need to do
WE WILL WORK FOR JUSTICE AND PEACE

When we are afraid
When we seek wisdom
WE WILL WALK IN THE LIGHT WHICH GOD GIVES US

When we are strong
When we need healing
WE WILL WALK IN THE LIGHT WHICH GOD GIVES US

When we are sad
When we are joyful
WE WILL WALK IN THE LIGHT WHICH GOD GIVES US

All our days
All of our pilgrimage
WE WILL WALK IN THE LIGHT THAT GOD GIVES US
WE WILL WALK SAFELY HOME.

Ruth Burgess

STORIES FROM AFRICA, 2005

George and Elizabeth

George and Elizabeth are in their mid-fifties; they are refugees from Congo living in Kenya, where they have been for the last fifteen years. They had four children. Their eldest girl, Susan, came back to stay with them after her husband died of AIDS five years ago. She had been sick on and off, then developed a tumour behind one of her eyes; in removing the tumour the eye was lost. In the final twelve months of her life she became increasingly sick and depressed and unable to care for her children. Susan died six months ago.

Hope, George and Elizabeth's youngest daughter, was a teacher and died of AIDS four weeks after giving birth to her third child. Her husband brought their three children to Elizabeth to care for; the baby is sickly and now nine months old. Hope's youngest son was found dead recently with some of his body parts removed. The people who killed him have not been found.

Elizabeth and George's eldest boy, Peter, is in the capital working for an NGO; he is married with three children. George and Elizabeth are at home with five grandchildren to care for.

Faith

Faith married Stephan seventeen years ago and they had six children. Three years ago, Stephan started losing weight and becoming tired after any exertion. He gradually became thinner and weaker and was unable to continue working. All of their savings were used up during this time, and they had to sell Stephan's bicycle and radio. Although Faith and Stephan tried many medicines, Stephan died two years ago.

After Stephan died, Faith had to move house and look for a job. She sent her three oldest children to live with her sister and kept the youngest children with her – a baby of six months, a boy of three and a girl of seven. She managed to get a scholarship for Susan, the oldest girl; her sister is paying for the two children in primary school; one is due to go to secondary school next year. In time, Faith was able to get a job as a 'house help'. While she works, Mary, who is now eight and not in school, cares for the two younger children; she also fetches water, cleans the house and prepares the meals.

Ruth

Ruth has four children of her own; they are 14, 10, 7 and 5. She also cares for two of her late brother's children; they are 9 and 7. Ruth's husband committed suicide four years ago for no obvious reason – he was in a good job, appeared to be in good health and seemed to have no particular worries. Five-year-old Anne has always been less robust than the others; she is the one to pick up any cold or sickness that is going around. After agonising over it for the last four years, Ruth went for an HIV test last month and has just received her results – she is negative.

Liz Paterson

OPEN OUR EYES

Open our eyes
to what we need to see
Open our ears
to what we need to hear
Open our minds
to what we need to know
Open our hearts
to what we need to bear
Open our hands
to what we need to give
Open our lives
to justice and love.

Ruth Burgess

BLESS YOUR PEOPLE

In Asia
In America
BLESS YOUR PEOPLE

In Europe
In Africa
BLESS YOUR PEOPLE

In Antarctica
In Australia
BLESS YOUR PEOPLE

In this place
In every place
BLESS YOUR PEOPLE

Bless your people with justice
BLESS YOUR PEOPLE WITH LOVE

Ruth Burgess

SUGGESTIONS FOR LITURGIES CONCERNING HIV/AIDS

Tell stories from around the world relating to HIV/AIDS. Search in the press or on websites for stories and current information.

Highlight the places the stories come from by using national flags, a large map of the world or a globe. Place lighted night lights on a world map or beside a globe as you pray for people in different countries.

Tie a red ribbon around the candle you light for the first Sunday in Advent and leave the ribbon there throughout the Advent season. Tie red ribbons around the candles you light at home.

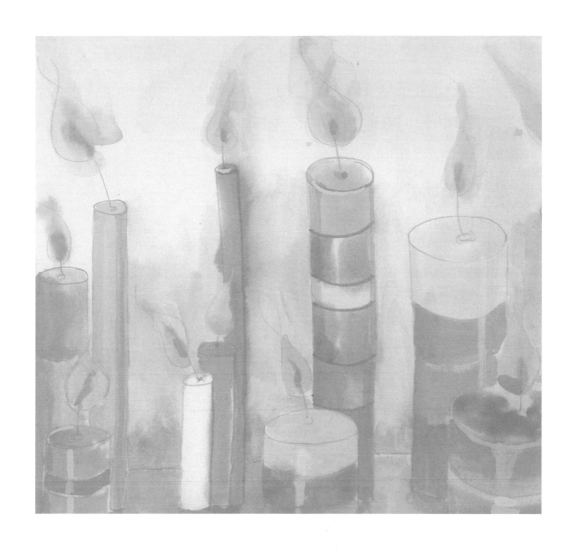

RESPONSES & BLESSINGS FOR THE SUNDAYS OF ADVENT

Cycles A, B, C

FIRST SUNDAY OF ADVENT
Cycle A
Is 2:1–5; Ps 122; Rom 13:11–14; Mt 24:37–44

Children and elders
Friends and strangers
WE COME TO GOD'S HOUSE

In good times and bad times
In joy and in sorrow
WE COME TO GOD'S HOUSE

Seeking God's wisdom
Asking God's blessing
WE COME TO GOD'S HOUSE

> In darkness and light
> WE WILL WALK WITH GOD

> In peace and in danger
> WE WILL WALK WITH GOD

> In living and dying
> WE WILL WALK WITH GOD

> We will live in God's light
> WE WILL WALK IN GOD'S WAYS

Blessing

We are pilgrims always
journeying homewards.
May God walk with us along the roads.

We look for peace
and we cry for justice.
May God make us peacemakers all our days.

We wait and long
for the coming of Jesus.
May God fill us with wonder and with great hope.

May the Bright God of Peace bless us,
Creator, Redeemer and Holy Spirit. AMEN

SECOND SUNDAY OF ADVENT
Cycle A
Is 11:1–10; Ps 72; Rom 15:4–9; Mt 3:1–12

God summons the innocent
God summons the guilty
GOD SUMMONS US WITH LOVE

God welcomes the poor
God welcomes the powerful
GOD WELCOMES US WITH LOVE

God judges the just
God judges the faithful
GOD JUDGES US WITH LOVE

> Like Abraham and Sarah laughing
> Like Jacob wrestling for a blessing
> KEEP US KEEPING ON

> Like Hannah praying in the temple
> Like Noah building boats in the wilderness
> KEEP US KEEPING ON

> Like Moses challenging injustice
> Like Joseph and Mary listening to angels
> KEEP US KEEPING ON

Blessing

We walk in the wilderness searching for meaning.
May God baptise us with mercy and fire.

We walk in the city thirsting for justice.
May God baptise us with integrity and hope.

We walk towards Bethlehem seeking a Saviour.
May God baptise us with holiness and joy.

And may the blessing of God, our Judge, Maker, Saviour and Holy Spirit,
come upon us now, and remain with us for ever. AMEN

THIRD SUNDAY OF ADVENT
Cycle A
Is 35:1–6,10; Ps 146; Jas 5:7–10; Mt 11:2–11

As farmers wait for rainfall
As prisoners wait for freedom
WE WAIT FOR THE COMING OF GOD

As exiles yearn for home
As peacemakers yearn for justice
WE LONG FOR THE COMING OF GOD

As travellers search for shelter
As disciples look for answers
WE PREPARE FOR THE COMING OF GOD

> Glory in the wilderness
> Glory in the wastelands
> SHOUT AND SING FOR JOY

> Strength for the weary
> Courage for the fearful
> SHOUT AND SING FOR JOY

> Shelter for the traveller
> Justice for the hungry
> SHOUT AND SING FOR JOY

Blessing

We have felt the sun and rainfall;
We have watched flowers blossom.
May God bless us in the turning of the earth.

We have read the story of Jesus;
We have found answers to our questions.
May God bless us in the hearing of the scriptures.

We have been met by the Holy Spirit;
Our lives have been changed and challenged.
May God bless us in the living of our days.

So may the God of Joy bless us, Planter, Nourisher and Fertilising Spirit,
this day and for evermore. AMEN

FOURTH SUNDAY OF ADVENT
Cycle A
Is 7:10–14; Ps 24; Rom1:1–7; Mt 1:18–24

God of creation
God of history
GOD IS HERE WITH US

God of mystery
God of blessing
GOD IS HERE WITH US

God in Jesus
God named Emmanuel
GOD IS HERE WITH US

> Beside us, beneath us,
> Behind us, before us,
> EMMANUEL

> Around us, amongst us,
> About us, ahead of us,
> EMMANUEL

> Leading us, protecting us,
> Challenging us, loving us,
> EMMANUEL

Blessing

We have walked in the wilderness;
We have waited and wondered.
May God bless us as we wait for a child's cry.

We have seen injustice;
We have brought God our questions.
May God bless us in darkness and light.

We have been bombarded with glitter and tinsel;
We have looked for a Saviour.
May God bless us as Christmas comes near.

Vulnerable God,
Risk-taker, Unborn Child and Holy Spirit,
bless us with wonder, and justice and hope. AMEN

FIRST SUNDAY OF ADVENT
Cycle B
Is 63:16–17; 64:1,3–8; Ps 80; 1 Cor 1:3–9; Mk 13:33–37

As stars to the maker
WE ARE THE WORK OF GOD'S HANDS

As plants to the gardener
WE ARE THE WORK OF GOD'S HANDS

As clay to the potter
WE ARE THE WORK OF GOD'S HANDS

> Be brave
> Be honest
> BE AWAKE TO INTEGRITY
>
> Be strong
> Be gentle
> BE AWAKE TO JUSTICE
>
> Be joyful
> Be humble
> BE AWAKE TO HOLINESS
>
> Be steady
> Be hopeful
> BE AWAKE TO LOVE

Blessing

We are looking for God in our world.
May we see what God wants us to see.

We are looking for God in our lives.
May we be who God wants us to be.

And may God our Shepherd, Protector, Awakener, and Holy Spirit,
bless us through these Advent days. AMEN

SECOND SUNDAY OF ADVENT
Cycle B
Is 40:1–5,9–11; Ps 85:2; Pet 3:8–14; Mk 1:1–8

High on the mountains
Someone is shouting
HERE COMES GOD

Justice is marching
Peace is following
HERE COMES GOD

Help is near
Shout for glory
HERE COMES GOD

> Through years and millennia
> Through days and moments
> WE ARE TRAVELLING HOME
>
> Trusting in promises
> Covered in mercy
> WE ARE TRAVELLING HOME
>
> Growing in holiness
> Heading for glory
> WE ARE TRAVELLING HOME

Blessing

We travel in time;
may God walk with us into eternity.

We travel in hope;
may God sing with us through the darkness.

We travel in wonder;
may God dance with us in holy joy.

So may the blessing of the God of glory,
Traveller, Storyteller, Dancer,
be in us today and every day. AMEN

THIRD SUNDAY OF ADVENT
Cycle B
Is 61:1–2,10–11; Lk 1:46–54; 1 Thes 5:16–24; Jn 1:6–8,19–28

God has called us
TO BRING GOOD NEWS TO THE POOR
TO LIVE WITH INTEGRITY

God has called us
TO HEAL THE BROKEN-HEARTED
TO BRING JUSTICE TO THE HUNGRY

God has called us
TO HOLD ON TO WHAT IS GOOD
TO AVOID EVERY FORM OF EVIL

The Spirit of God is in us
WE ARE PEOPLE OF GOD

> Be happy
> Be holy
> REJOICE IN GOD

> Be brave
> Love justice
> REJOICE IN GOD

> Be merciful
> Walk wisely
> REJOICE IN GOD

> Be good
> Avoid evil
> REJOICE IN GOD

Blessing

May God wrap us in integrity,
Clothe us in salvation,
And adorn us with beauty and joy.

And may the blessing of God,
Protector, Perfecter and Spirit of Joy,
surround us all our nights and days. AMEN

FOURTH SUNDAY OF ADVENT

Cycle B
2 Sam 7:1–16; Ps 89; Rom 16:25–27; Lk 1:26–38

An ancient promise is coming true
GOD'S LOVE LASTS FOR EVER

A secret mystery is being revealed
GOD'S LOVE LASTS FOR EVER

A little child will soon be born
GOD'S LOVE LASTS FOR EVER

> God of promise
> God of wisdom
> WE WILL WAIT WITH YOU
>
> God of justice
> God of integrity
> WE WILL WALK WITH YOU
>
> God of mystery
> God of glory
> WE WILL LAUGH WITH YOU

Blessing

We have heard the words of prophets.
May we recognise God's truth.

We have heard the words of angels.
May we recognise God's joy.

We have heard the words of promise.
May we recognise God's love.

And so may God bless us,
Mystery of creation, Child in the manger, Holy Spirit of glory,
and may we welcome and walk in the promises of God. AMEN

FIRST SUNDAY OF ADVENT
Cycle C
Jer 33:14–16; Ps 25; 1 Thes 3:12–4:2; Lk 21:25–28,34–36

Faithful and wise
Full of integrity
GOD IS OUR FRIEND

Honest and true
Keeper of promises
GOD IS OUR FRIEND

Strong and upright
Lover of justice
GOD IS OUR FRIEND

> In the daytime
> Through the night time
> KEEP US ON THE RIGHT PATH
>
> In our learning
> In our growing
> KEEP US ON THE RIGHT PATH
>
> In our living
> In our dying
> KEEP US ON THE RIGHT PATH

Blessing

We seek God's ways;
may we walk in God's truth.

We seek God's friendship;
may we live in God's justice.

We trust in God's promises;
may we delight in God's love.

May the God of pilgrimage,
Maker, Traveller, Spirit of adventure and joy,
bless us and encourage us all the days of our journey home. AMEN

SECOND SUNDAY OF ADVENT
Cycle C
Baruch 5:1–9; Ps 126; Phil 1:4–6,8–11; Lk 3:1–6

Sowing and reaping
Coming and going
GOD IS WORKING IN US

Weeping and singing
Hoping and praying
GOD IS WORKING IN US

Travelling and resting
Learning and loving
GOD IS WORKING IN US

> In our watching
> In our waiting
> God is alive in us
> AND WE ARE GLAD

> In our questioning
> In our hoping
> God is alive in us
> AND WE ARE GLAD

> In our dreaming
> In our dancing
> God is alive in us
> AND WE ARE GLAD

> In our travelling
> In our homecoming
> God is alive in us
> AND WE ARE GLAD

Blessing

God have mercy on your people,
baptise us in wisdom

and clothe us in integrity;
wrap us in the beauty of your love.

And may the God of mercy bless us,
Deliverer, Lover and Breath of life. AMEN

THIRD SUNDAY OF ADVENT
Cycle C
Zeph 3:14–18; Is 12:2–6; Phil 4:4–7; Lk 3:10–18

God is among us
God is within us
GOD IS DANCING WITH JOY

God is our strength
God is our Saviour
GOD IS DANCING WITH JOY

God is our peace
God is our festivity
GOD IS DANCING WITH JOY

> What must we do?
> We must pray faithfully
> WE MUST LIVE IN LOVE

> What must we do?
> We must share our possessions
> WE MUST LIVE IN LOVE

> What must we do?
> We must act justly
> WE MUST LIVE IN LOVE

Blessing

We know that God wants us to be happy.
May we enjoy God's love gladly and with great hope.

We know that God wants us to be holy.
May we drink of God's love deeply and with great joy.

God of the Dance, Storyteller, Joy of our joy,
bless us with laughter and glory
in all the light and darkness of our days. AMEN

FOURTH SUNDAY OF ADVENT
Cycle C
Mic 5:1–4; Ps 80; Heb 10:5–10; Lk 1:39–44

In Bethlehem
Will be born a Saviour
SING FOR JOY

The God of Hosts
Will live among us
SHOUT FOR JOY

Love and laughter
Will leap within us
JUMP AND DANCE FOR JOY

> In towns and villages
> In tower blocks and terraces
> CHRIST IS WAITING TO BE BORN
>
> In palaces and shanty-towns
> In high streets and back-streets
> CHRIST IS WAITING TO BE BORN
>
> In the vastness of the universe
> In the intimacy of our hearts
> CHRIST IS WAITING TO BE BORN
>
> Come, Lord Jesus
> COME INTO OUR HOMES
> COME INTO OUR LIVES
> COME AND STAY.

Blessing

Let your face shine on us and bless us;
God of Hosts, Maker, Saviour and Holy Spirit,
root your justice in us all our days. AMEN

Ruth Burgess

THE CATS' ADVENT
CALENDAR

DECEMBER 1ST

We have three cats at Coleg y Groes* – Pod, Jemima Socs and Tomos. The last two are sister and brother. Pod is a small, three-legged tortoiseshell who is nine years their senior and 'top cat'. Jemima Socs and Tomos thought that their first Christmas was wonderful. They especially enjoyed the wrapping paper and sitting on the roof of the crib pretending to be angels. They realised that something was different without really knowing why. So the next year Pod saw it as her duty, as senior cat, to fill them in and to tell them the stories that cats have passed down through the ages. They decided one day that they would like to share their stories with their human friends. As paws are not really suitable for computer keyboards (though very good for lots of more important things!) they enlisted our help in producing this Advent calendar. You will probably find it easier to turn pages than they do, so do look up the Bible stories when you come to the references.

Pod, Jemima Socs and Tomos will start the story tomorrow. It's a very good story, really good news – and you know how good that is. (See Proverbs 25:25)

* *Coleg y Groes is a retreat house in Wales.*

DECEMBER 2ND
The Egyptian cat's story

Egypt was a very good place to live about 3,500 years ago. We cats were looked up to and valued. In fact, we were so valued that our humans thought we were gods! They got that wrong of course – but it made for a very comfortable life. Those of us who weren't into the god thing were expected to work for our living. But the work was important. We had the job of guarding the nation's food – the best of jobs, as it meant that we got to chase mice all day (when we weren't sleeping it off in a nice cosy corner of the grain store). We were especially fortunate. Cats in countries round about were having a very hard time. There had been a famine for seven years and food was so scarce that even mice were in short supply (after all, they have to eat too). But we were all right. God (the real one) had provided just the right man to sort things out. He was called Joseph. He had arrived in Egypt because his brothers had sold him, they hated him so much. He had had a very hard time. But Joseph knew God was with him, even in the really bad times. And Joseph became the person who saved not only Egypt from famine, but his own family too. They all ended up in Egypt. And we cats had a wonderful time. (Read Genesis 41:49 and you'll see how much food we had.)

DECEMBER 3RD

The Egyptian cat's story continued

I was a kitten in Egypt many years after Joseph. I was being trained for a position in the royal household. My human was one of the royal princesses. I worked hard at becoming indispensable to her. She liked to have me around whatever she was doing. I was having a very good life. So it happened that one day when she went down to the river for her daily bath, I went along too. (A tongue is so much more convenient I always think!) I was enjoying stretching in the sun and looking attractive, when my ears pricked up. There was a sound just like a kitten. A kitten in the water! I ran to the princess and tried my best to make her do something about it. After all, nobody could expect me to go into the river. Eventually she sent her slaves to investigate. And there it was, not a kitten but a human baby. She took him home and called him Moses. We became very good friends. I didn't realise at the time how important my excellent hearing had been! (Read the story in Exodus 2:1–10.)

DECEMBER 4TH

The Egyptian cat's story continued

Moses became an important man. God got him to organise the great crowd of people that had grown out of the 70 or so who had originally arrived with Joseph's father and brothers. The Egyptians had made them slaves, but Moses led them to freedom. He took me with him of course. I had no intention of missing out on the adventure. And, to tell you the truth, I was very fond of Moses. He needed a good cat to keep an eye on him and to help him unwind. Humans seem to find it quite difficult to relax completely. We cats have, of course, perfected the art. We're good at finding something in every situation to amuse and distract us. Moses really needed to keep a sense of humour. He had grumbling Israelites to coax along and keep on the straight and narrow. He and God together produced lists of rules and good advice, and a wonderful moveable God-place. It was all very exciting. But you would be surprised at how quickly the humans ignored the rules and stopped being amazed at the God-place. It's a good job God didn't forget them so quickly! (You can read about it in Exodus 20:1–12.)

DECEMBER 5TH

The Egyptian cat's story continued

You don't need me to tell you how important food is to us cats! Meals are obviously just about the most important events of every day. I think God must agree with us. Think of the Passover for instance. There we all were, humans and animals, waiting to see if Pharaoh was at last going to say 'Yes' and let us go free. Bags were packed in readiness. We knew we would have to make a quick getaway. And there was Moses, passing on God's instructions for a final meal – a special event, no quick mouthful of mouse and eat the rest on the run. We had to prepare this meal properly. Maybe he knew that, for the next 40 years, food was going to be available, but boring. One of the joys of any cat's life is the adventure of sampling the strange tastes of human food. I know manna was 'food from heaven' and miraculous and all that. But you can get tired of even miraculous food when it's the same every day! I looked forward to the wonderful country we were travelling to. Honey … and milk! (See Exodus 3:17)

DECEMBER 6TH

The Egyptian cat's story continued

He was a wonderful man, my Moses. The amount of hassle he had with the Israelites! Sometimes he just didn't know what to do. I tried my best to help and comfort and to amuse and encourage him. Sometimes humans can be so stupid! But Moses was usually very patient with them (not always – I soon learnt when to keep out of his way) and he never gave up on God. He was very old when he died. He never managed to get to the wonderful land of milk and honey after all. But he did see it. Everyone was very sad when he died, even if they had found him difficult some of the time. There was no one like him. (Deuteronomy 34:10–12)

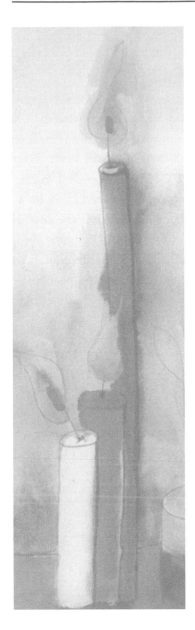

DECEMBER 7TH

The prophet's cat's story

Time passed … It passed in a very messy way, sometimes in a rather boring way, and, now and again, in a very exciting way. There were wars and famines and victories and parties. Some very odd things happened – there was the strange time when the Philistines, who attacked Israel with boring regularity, gave God an offering of golden mice (honestly! See 1 Samuel 6:4). Very pretty no doubt – but what use are gold mice! The Israelites were good at giving God gifts too – some of their sacrifices would have fed my family and me for years! But they weren't so good at doing what God said. That's where my human came in. He was a prophet. No, nothing to do with profit – there wasn't much money in the job. In fact, as far as food went, it was often a case of every cat fending for itself. But we managed. And the really good thing was that my human was almost as much in touch with God as we cats usually are. He knew about being very still and just waiting and listening … and he knew about enjoying God too. Sometimes I wonder what is wrong with humans that they seem to enjoy life so little. There is so much to smell and discover and chase. Some humans don't seem to know that God is around at all! My human was very good at talking as well as being quiet. I take after him a little, people say, but of course the truth of the matter is that he takes after me!

DECEMBER 8TH

The prophet's cat's story continued

One of the really important things my human, and others like him, spoke about and wrote about was this: They told people that one day God was going to send a very special person. He was going to grow up on Earth, just like the rest of us. But he was to be special. No one was quite sure what that meant, though they had some hints about it. And they didn't know when this was to happen. They called him Messiah (it means 'anointed one'). When he came things would change, they said. We weren't sure how, but we all started to daydream and sometimes the daydreams turned into the sort of hope that keeps you going when the mice seem to be in hiding and the house is cold. One of the prophets, Micah, discovered where he would be born. Read about it in Micah 5:2. We thought that was quite suitable. After all, our greatest king ever came from the same place. (See 1 Samuel 16:1–15)

DECEMBER 9TH

The prophet's cat's story continued

One of the greatest prophets was a man called Isaiah. A long collection of writings has his name. He wrote about the Messiah. But he wrote about other things too. He looked even further ahead to a time of judgement at the end of everything. He was a great man – though I sometimes wonder whether he could have heard everything accurately. His book says that God will condemn those who eat mice! (Isaiah 66:17) But people say it wasn't actually Isaiah who wrote that section – and I must say I agree with them. It must have been a very minor sort of prophet who was still learning to listen!

DECEMBER 10TH

The prophet's cat's story continued

Isaiah didn't just write about banning mice. Try reading Isaiah 11:1–9. It's full of clues about the Messiah's Kingdom. Note that cats are included in this. Feline experts agree that the reference to 'the most honoured in the cat world' (verse 6) must represent us all. You must always remember that – especially when you have one of those days when your humans don't seem to understand, the dog next door chases you, and you are sick in the wrong place.

DECEMBER 11TH

The prophet's cat's story continued

You'll soon discover that there are lots of lights around at Christmas time. Humans put them in unlikely places, such as on a small tree inside the house. A word of advice: You can go up to them and look at them and even pat them gently – your humans will say things like, 'Look, isn't he sweet' and make a great fuss over you and you'll enjoy that – but, whatever you do, don't try to chase them if they flash. And never try to kill them. There is something very strange about these sorts of lights and they can hurt you quite badly – they sort of snap back. Learn from our experience; it's just not worth it.

Humans light the small lights to help them celebrate the Messiah, who was a greater sort of light; not just a light for one room but Light for the whole world. A changing-your-life light, not a snapping-back sort. (Read about it in Isaiah 9:2.)

DECEMBER 12TH

The prophet's cat's story continued

Sometimes the prophets wrote very strange words. We cats have spent many hours wondering what they may mean. Look at Isaiah 53, for example. You would think that this Messiah would be strong and powerful and great, wouldn't you? But this chapter is all about someone who suffers. Things seem to be going very wrong for him. Yet, at the end of the chapter, there is honour and hope …Very strange. We had to wait for a long time to discover what it meant. My master never knew. Isaiah didn't either, at least not fully. But it's a good chapter for when you are having a hard time. We understand it better now, of course.

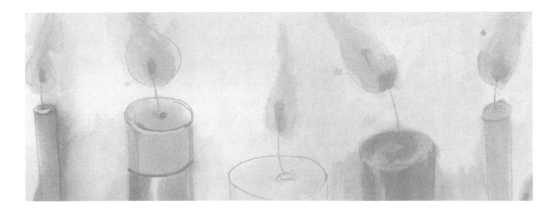

DECEMBER 13TH

The prophet's cat's story continued

Time passed. A long time. We kept hoping. Nothing seemed to be happening, except the usual stuff about trying to obey God and not always getting it right, and sometimes getting it very wrong, and sometimes not even trying … In the temple we sang a song: 'O rest in the Lord, wait patiently for him …' Humans are not very good at resting and waiting, in my experience. We cats are much better! (The waiting patiently song is Psalm 37.)

DECEMBER 14TH

Mary's cat's story

My story is a really exciting one. I'm the cat who had the great privilege of being there when the waiting ended. For many lifetimes we had been waiting. Sometimes we almost forgot what we were waiting for. But then someone would remember that God had promised the Messiah. Or, to be more accurate, God would remind us and someone would start to listen properly to what God was saying and then remind the rest of us.

We cats are very good at waiting. We like to be still and contemplate the great truths of God, the universe and everything. Some humans think we're asleep – but of course they are mistaken! But even we began to wonder if God was ever going to do anything about it. Then, one day, something happened. It was like being given the key to a mystery. (See Ephesians 1:9–10)

DECEMBER 15TH

Mary's cat's story continued

This is what happened: We, the family and I, had been looking forward to a wedding; young Mary was betrothed to Joseph. He was a much respected member of the village, a carpenter with his own business. Rather older than Mary, but we all thought he was quite a catch. Mary was certainly very happy. She was so young, only a teenager, but trying to grow up very quickly. Then, one day, as she was getting on with some house-work, someone arrived. I felt my fur shiver. There was something so strange about this person. Scary, but good too. He bent down to stroke me and it was like being stroked by lightning. I ran to Mary. She obviously needed my protection! He introduced himself. 'Gabriel,' he said. 'My name is Gabriel.' The story is written down (Luke

1:26–38) so I won't go into the detail. You can read that. When Gabriel had gone Mary sat very still. I jumped onto her lap but she didn't really notice I was there. I didn't blame her. Her world had just been turned upside down. Nothing would ever be the same again for the whole world, let alone the two of us.

DECEMBER 16TH

Mary's cat's story continued

My comfortable life became much less comfortable. Within a few days Mary managed to persuade everyone that it would be a really good idea for her to visit her cousin Elizabeth, who lived in the south of the country at Jerusalem. It was obvious that Elizabeth would be glad of such a visit. They were very close, Mary and Elizabeth, although there was a big age gap. Elizabeth was more like an auntie than a cousin. She, Elizabeth, had been discovering about life being turned upside down herself. After years and years of marriage, at long last she was going to have a baby. There was something very marvellous and rather odd about that too! I think Mary thought Elizabeth might be able to help her believe in what had happened to her. After all Elizabeth had had some practice in believing impossible things. She must have been glad to have Mary to chat to. Her husband had been slower in getting his mind around what was happening to them and, as a result, Gabriel had declared that he was to be dumb until their baby was born, and he was. Gabriel had been involved there too. He gets around does Gabriel! Mary and Elizabeth must have talked and talked and talked. Meanwhile, I was missing her. I only had her smell to remember her by. (The story is in Luke 1:5–25,39–56.)

DECEMBER 17TH

Mary's cat's story continued

There was such a rumpus when Mary came back home from Elizabeth's. She came in, full of the news of Elizabeth and Zechariah's baby boy. But no one took much notice of that. For it was beginning to be obvious that Mary herself was pregnant. After not seeing her for three months everyone noticed. It was a very difficult time. Joseph, her fiancé, was shattered. He started to work out how to cancel the wedding with the least possible fuss. I couldn't understand at first why Mary didn't explain about Gabriel and God and the Messiah. Then I started to understand that Joseph wouldn't be able to believe it. I didn't know what to do and wasn't able to purr for days. Then, suddenly, it all changed. Joseph started coming round again. He was very gentle and attentive to Mary. The neighbours were amazed. But I heard the two of them talking and realised that God had fixed it. Joseph understood now. They talked in wonder about one of Isaiah's prophecies that was about to come true. (You can find it in Matthew 1:22–23.)

DECEMBER 18ᵀᴴ

Mary's cat's story continued

Then, just as I was looking forward to a small human to play with, everyone was thrown into confusion again. The powers that be, Rome and all that, decided to revise the tax system. Joseph, along with everyone else, had to go to his family's town, right at the other end of the country. I could never work out why people couldn't stay where they were to sign the piece of paper. But that's the government for you. There was no way that Joseph was going anywhere without Mary. So they set out together. The baby was due anytime. We were all so worried. I was so miserable and went to hide under the bed. Then I suddenly thought of something. They were going to Bethlehem. And that was just where one of the prophets had said it would happen. The Messiah, I mean. Gosh! So I thought I'd better go along with whatever God was doing and, meanwhile, get on with my own job of mouse-catching. (The story is in Luke 2:1–5.)

DECEMBER 19TH

The stable cat's story

I am the stable cat. It's a good life. Not as soft and comfortable as a house cat's, but the stable is quite presentable and I have a warm nest in one of the least draughty corners. There are lots of mice around. And the freedom is worth any discomfort. I do value my independence and quiet life. So I wasn't best pleased when, just as I had settled down for a snooze after a good mousing session, the human from the inn next door burst in with two people to stay the night in my stable. It was obvious that my quiet life was over for some time. The woman was about to have a baby. We all know what a noise kittens can make – and human babies are worse! I couldn't imagine why they weren't in one of the inns. (Luke 2:7 explains.)

DECEMBER 20TH

The stable cat's story continued

But, in spite of myself, as the night went on, I began to feel for that young couple. It must have been hard to have what was obviously a first child in such conditions. Much as I enjoy my stable I can see that it is not the ideal place for a human baby to be born. But the girl made no fuss. And in the darkest part of the night the baby was born. A boy. She cuddled him and she and the man looked as if they had been given the whole Earth. The place was full of the smell of joy and new baby. (The story is in Luke 2:1–8.)

DECEMBER 21ST

The stable cat's story continued

Strange things happened that night. I was busy snuggling up to Mary (I'd found out her name by then) to keep her warm. There was much to think about and do with a new baby. Joseph was busy trying to make the place more comfortable and fixing up a feeding trough as a makeshift cradle. Looking back, maybe I did hear singing, outside and far away. But I didn't pay any attention to it. Out on the hillside a few shepherds were visited by angels. Not just one this time, but a whole choir of them. (Luke 2:8–14)

DECEMBER 22ND

The stable cat's story continued

The four of us had just settled down. We were very tired. I must have dozed off for a minute or two. Suddenly, the stable was full of men. Rough and rather smelly men. Shepherds.

Joseph jumped up, ready to protect Mary and the baby. I jumped quickly to a safe place. But we need not have worried. They were very quiet. Almost shy. They muttered to one another. 'It's just as the angel said. It's the Messiah. It's David's Son.' Then they pulled themselves together and told us all about the angels and the singing and the great light, and the angel's message. This baby was such a special baby. I was glad I'd been disturbed. It was worth it to be in on such a wonderful happening. God becoming a baby! Not quite a kitten, but very nearly! I purred very loudly. 'See, even the cat knows what has happened tonight,' one of the shepherds said. (Luke 2:15–20)

DECEMBER 23RD

The stable cat's story continued

The shepherds told everybody about the special baby, so Mary and Joseph had lots of visitors. Then things quietened down again. After a few days, Joseph found a small house where they could live until the baby was old enough to travel. I thought I would be glad to get back to my independent life. I hadn't had a good mousing night ever since the baby had been born. But as they left I suddenly felt I wouldn't miss the old life after all. Not if I could be with this special baby. So I followed them to their new home. I wondered if I'd be welcome. After all I'm nothing special to look at. I've had a few fights so there are bits of fur and ear missing now. But Mary said, 'Oh, good!', when I turned up. And the baby gurgled and held out his hands to me.

After a few months I'd almost forgotten about the strange happenings in the stable; I was a responsible house cat now. Then, one day, people began to talk about a new star that was shining very brightly in the night sky. I went out to have a look. It almost seemed to have settled just over our house. Other people thought so, too. (Matthew 2:1–10)

DECEMBER 24TH

The stable cat's story continued

The people that came were almost as good as the star! People from countries I'd never heard of, talking in different languages and wearing strange clothes and riding on odd animals. They said they had come because of the star. There, in the night sky, they had read the birth announcement about this baby. I can't imagine how they had managed that. The books that people read are difficult enough as far as I can see. But reading stars! We all reckoned that God must have helped them. They said that King Herod had helped them, but from what I have heard about him that seemed even less likely than stars! And I was proved right. The visitors came into our little house and filled it. They gave three special presents to the new baby. I didn't think they were as useful as mice, but Mary and Joseph were very polite. And then they did something odder than all the other things. They knelt down and worshipped that baby, just as if he were God himself. Everything went very quiet for a long moment and I sat very still too. And, gradually, I realised that they were right to do that. So I went and rolled over on my back to worship him too. And he laughed with joy. (Matthew 2:11)

DECEMBER 25TH

Pod's Christmas message

We hope you have enjoyed the stories of our ancestors. Enjoy the wrapping paper – and there are some rather special smells and tastes about too!

Even our own very special humans find it hard to understand our world completely. But we cats can understand that today is very very special (John 1:14) and that cats and human beings and even mice can all enjoy it.

Pod, with a little help from Margaret Harvey

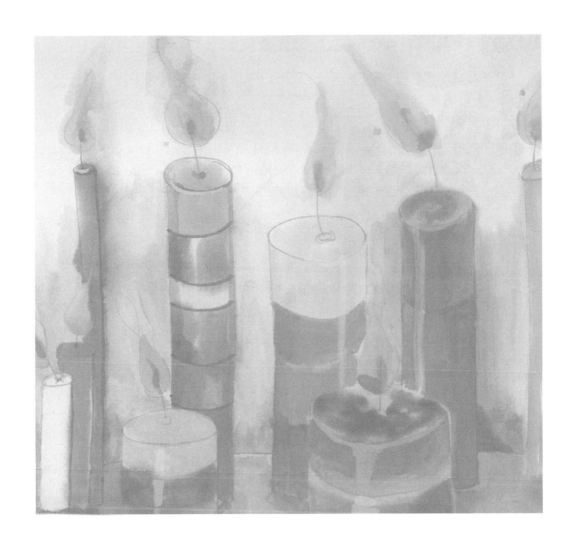

ADVENT CANDLE
CEREMONIES

WATCH AND WAIT AND PRAY

An opening for worship (for all four Sundays in Advent)

Call to worship

Leader: In this season of Advent, we are here to watch and wait and pray for the coming of light into the world. We long for the day when the things of darkness – selfishness and greed, suffering and oppression – shall be no more.

Light candle/s

ALL: LORD, BY YOUR PRESENCE,
LIGHT UP THE PAST
THAT WE MIGHT LEARN FROM IT WITH THANKFULNESS.

LIGHT UP THE PRESENT
THAT WE MIGHT LIVE IN IT WITH LOVE.

LIGHT UP THE FUTURE
THAT WE MIGHT PREPARE FOR IT IN HOPE.

AS WE WATCH AND WAIT AND PRAY,
MAY WE BE ALWAYS READY TO ENCOUNTER THE LORD
WHO IS ALREADY AND ALWAYS WITH US. AMEN

Song: Advent is a time of waiting
(Tune: Westminster Abbey)

Advent is a time of waiting
for the life that is to be.
When the Christ, by prophets promised,
sits enthroned on Mary's knee,
human in the way that we are;
come to earth for you and me.

Choirs of angels are rehearsing,
'Glory to our God on high.'
Shepherds in the field are watching
where their bleating charges lie.
Distant magi, waiting, restless,
scan the dark mysterious sky.

Hope is all our theme for Advent,
hope for all the human race.
All our hope on God is founded,
God who shows a human face.
God who made the Earth and planets
now appears in time and space.

Josie Smith

GIVE LIGHT, GIVE HOPE
Responses for lighting Advent candles

First Sunday of Advent: Hope for all God's people

We light this candle for all God's people,
struggling to be bearers of hope
in a troubled world.
GOD, AS WE WAIT FOR YOUR PROMISE,
GIVE LIGHT, GIVE HOPE.

Second Sunday of Advent: The prophets

We light this candle for all God's prophets,
confronting justice and restoring the dream
of a world of freedom and peace.
GOD, AS WE WAIT FOR YOUR PROMISE,
GIVE LIGHT, GIVE HOPE.

Third Sunday of Advent: John the Baptist

We light this candle for all God's messengers,
preparing the way for change,
signs pointing to a new age to come.
GOD, AS WE WAIT FOR YOUR PROMISE,
GIVE LIGHT, GIVE HOPE.

Fourth Sunday of Advent: Mary

We light this candle for all God-bearers,
saying 'yes' to God's challenge,
accepting the pain and joy of an unknown future.
GOD, AS WE WAIT FOR YOUR PROMISE,
GIVE LIGHT, GIVE HOPE.

Christmas Day: The birth of Christ

We light this candle for the newborn Christ,
reawakening hope and faith –
the Word embodied for our time.
GOD, AS WE RECEIVE YOUR PROMISE,
YOU ARE LIGHT, YOU ARE HOPE.

Jan Berry

A CANDLE BURNS
Prayers for lighting Advent candles

1st Sunday in Advent

A candle burns,
the sign of our hope.
God of hope,
come to us again this Advent.
May your hope live within us,
burning as a light in our lives.

2nd Sunday in Advent

A candle burns,
the sign of your Word.
God of the prophets,
come to us again this Advent.
May your Word be a lamp to our feet
and a light on our path.

3rd Sunday in Advent

A candle burns,
the sign of our faith.
God of the Baptising One,
come to us again this Advent.
May we have a faith that renews our lives.
May we live in the light of your promises.

4th Sunday in Advent

A candle burns,
the sign of your love.
God of Mary,
come to us again this Advent.
May the light of your love
be born anew in us.

Christmas Day

A candle burns,
the sign of your presence.
God amongst us,
born as one of us,
may we live in the light of your presence,
the Light who gives life to all.

David Hamflett

SIGNPOSTS THROUGH ADVENT

Prayers for lighting Advent candles

1st Sunday in Advent

A candle burns,
the first marker of our Advent journey.
As we set out,
may we travel hopefully.
As we set out,
God of journeys, travel with us.

2nd Sunday in Advent

A candle burns,
the second marker of our Advent journey.
As we continue,
may we travel faithfully.
As we continue,
God of journeys, speak to us.

3rd Sunday in Advent

A candle burns,
the third marker of our Advent journey.
As we continue,
may we travel expectantly.
As we continue,
God of journeys, guide our footsteps.

4th Sunday in Advent

A candle burns,
the fourth marker of our Advent journey.
As we continue,
may we travel joyfully.
As we continue,
God of journeys, draw us to our journey's end.

Christmas Day

A candle burns,
the last marker of our Advent journey.
As we arrive at our journey's end,
may we arrive with wonder and worship.
As we arrive at our journey's end,
God of journeys, welcome us.

David Hamflett

THE CANDLES OF ADVENT

On the first Sunday in Advent

As the first candle of Advent is lit someone says:

One candle to remind us of the prophets, who believed in God during dark days, and looked forward to the coming of Christ.

Someone reads: The people who walked in darkness have seen a great light. They lived in a land of shadows, but now light is shining on them. *(Isaiah 9:2)*

LIVING GOD, WE THANK YOU FOR FAITHFUL PEOPLE OF EVERY AGE. WE PRAY THAT WE, TOO, MAY HAVE FAITH, IN SPITE OF THE DARKNESS OF OUR TIMES, AND MAY LOOK FOR THE COMING OF JESUS INTO OUR WORLD. AMEN

On the second Sunday in Advent

As two candles are lit someone says:

One candle to remind us of the prophets, the second for John the Baptist, who called people to change their way of living to prepare for the coming of Christ.

Someone reads: The light shines in the darkness and the darkness has never put it out. God sent his messenger, a man named John, who came to tell people about the light, so that all should hear the message and believe. *(John 1:5–7)*

DISTURBING GOD, WE THANK YOU FOR THE WITNESS OF JOHN THE BAPTIST. HELP US TO BE OPEN TO THE CHANGING POWER OF YOUR LOVE, AND TO BE TRUE WITNESSES TO THE POWER OF JESUS IN OUR LIVES. AMEN

On the third Sunday in Advent

As three candles are lit someone says:

One candle to remind us of the prophets, the second for John the Baptist, and the third for Mary, who gladly responded to the call of God.

Someone reads: 'I am the Lord's servant,' said Mary; 'may it happen to me as you have said.' *(Luke1:38)*

STARTLING GOD, WE THANK YOU FOR THE JOYFUL OBEDIENCE OF MARY. WE ASK YOU TO FILL US WITH YOUR GRACE, SO THAT WE, TOO, MAY ACCEPT YOUR CALL, AND REJOICE IN YOUR SALVATION. AMEN

On the fourth Sunday in Advent

As four candles are lit someone says:

One candle to remind us of the prophets, the second for John the Baptist, the third for Mary, and the fourth for us, as we join with them in looking for the coming of Jesus.

Someone reads: God will give you a sign, a young woman who is pregnant will have a son and will name him Immanuel, which means 'God is with us'. *(Isaiah 7:14)*

GRACIOUS GOD, AS YOU CAME TO THOSE WHO HAVE GONE BEFORE US, YOU COME TO US NOW IN JESUS. HELP US TO RECOGNISE YOU IN THOSE AROUND US AND TO CARE FOR OUR NEIGHBOURS AS WE DO FOR OURSELVES. AMEN

On Christmas Day

As four candles and the central candle are lit someone says:

One candle to remind us of the prophets, the second for John the Baptist, the third for Mary, and the fourth for us. Now, the central candle for Jesus, born today. Jesus is the light of the world.

Someone reads: Mary gave birth to her first son, wrapped him in strips of cloth, and laid him in a manger – there was no room for them to stay in the inn. *(Luke 2:7)*

LOVING GOD, WE THANK YOU FOR THE BIRTH OF JESUS CHRIST OUR SAVIOUR. MAY WE ALWAYS WELCOME HIM INTO OUR COMMUNITY, OUR HOMES, OUR LIVES.

TODAY WE CELEBRATE HIS BIRTH WITH GREAT JOY. AMEN

Adapted by Ruth Burgess from material written by the Notting Hill Group Ministry in 1968 (Geoffrey Ainger, Norwyn Denny, David Mason)

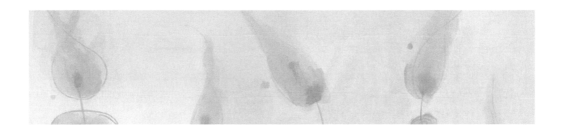

ONE RED CANDLE

(Tune: Frère Jacques)
Each line of this song is repeated.

One red candle
Burning slow
Advent weeks of waiting
Three to go

Mary's waiting
Joseph too
Waiting for the baby
Coming soon

Two red candles
Burning slow
Advent weeks of waiting
Two to go

Wise men watching
For a star
Going on a journey
In the dark

Three red candles
Burning slow
Advent weeks of waiting
One to go

Shepherds listening
In the night
Will they hear the angels
Sing tonight?

Four red candles
Burning slow
Soon it will be Christmas
Not long now

We are waiting
Watching too
Soon it will be Christmas
For me and you

One white candle
Christmas Day
Welcome, baby Jesus
Come and stay

Ruth Burgess

(Each line of this song could be sung by a cantor and repeated
back by a group. You might like to sing a new verse for each
week of Advent. Figures (Mary, Joseph, the wise men ...) could
be added to a nativity scene during the song, as suggested by
the verses.)

COME AND LIGHT THE CANDLES

Advent candle song

(Tune: Glenfinlas)

Come and light the candles on the Advent ring,
scattering the darkness till the world shall sing.

We are all God's people, waiting in this place,
hoping that in Jesus we shall see God's face.

Prophet voices speaking clear, like a burning flame,
making sure our world will never be the same.

John the Baptist telling us God wants to forgive,
calling us to change the way we work and live.

Mary, full of courage, echoing God's yes,
going on the journey God will greatly bless.

Jesus in the midst of us, filling us with joy,
giving us the life which nothing can destroy.

Janet Morley

SHINE A LIGHT

Words and music: Brian Woodcock

Verse 3, 4, 5

Shine an - o - ther light! __ Shine an - o - ther light! __ Shine an -

Verse 2

Shine an o - ther! Shine an o - ther! Shine an -

Verse 1

Shine a light! Shine a light!
Shine a light for the prophets of the world.
Shine a light for the beacons that burn in every age
    till his kingdom come
    and his will is done
    and the glory of the Lord is revealed.

Shine another! Shine another!
Shine a light in the darkness of the world.
It's for John the Baptist, and those who pave the way
    till his kingdom come …

Shine another light! Shine another light!
Shine a light at the heart of all the world.
And the third is for Mary, and all that gives him birth
    till his kingdom come …

Shine a dozen lights! Shine a thousand lights!
Let them shine from the hilltops of the world.
They're for you; they're for me;
they're for all who wait for him
    till his kingdom come …

Come into the light! Come into the light!
Jesus Christ is the light of all the world.
And his day has arrived, and the darkness is no more,
    for his kingdom's come
    and his will is done
    and the glory of the Lord is revealed.

Brian Woodcock

LITURGIES AND PRAYER
PRACTICES FOR ADVENT

ADVENT IS FOR EVERYONE
Four all-age liturgies and activities for Advent

ADVENT ONE

Opening responses

In the beginning, when it was very dark, God said: 'Let there be light.'
AND THERE WAS LIGHT.
God's light goes on shining in the darkness
AND THE DARKNESS HAS NEVER PUT IT OUT.

Bible reading

Jesus said: 'You are like light for the whole world. A city built on a hill cannot be hid.
No one lights a lamp and puts it under a bowl; instead he puts it on the lamp-stand,
where it gives light to everyone in the house. In the same way, your light must shine
before others, so that they will see the good things that you do and praise God in
heaven.' *(Matthew 5:14–16, adapted)*

Prayers

We thank God for the people whose lives have been like light in dark places …

God, in your mercy,
HEAR OUR PRAYER

We pray for ourselves, that God's light may shine in us …

God, in your mercy,
HEAR OUR PRAYER. AMEN

Song: Sing a song about light (e.g. This little light of mine; Walk in the light; Jesus bids
us shine; Shine, Jesus shine; Give me oil in my lamp)

Closing responses

The light of God
TO LEAD US AND MAKE US UNAFRAID.
The power of God
TO PROTECT US AND MAKE US STRONG.
The joy of God

TO HEAL US AND MAKE US HAPPY.
The grace of God
TO BLESS US AND KEEP US LOVING.
NOW AND EVERMORE. AMEN

Note: Candles could be used during this service – at the beginning and end, during the prayers.

Discussion and activities: Researching and sharing stories of prophets, ancient and modern; candle-making.

ADVENT TWO

Opening responses

Someone is shouting:
GET READY FOR GOD.
Someone is whispering:
GET READY FOR GOD.
Someone is singing:
GET READY FOR GOD.
God is coming soon.

Bible reading

The word of God came to John, son of Zechariah, in the desert. So John went throughout the whole territory of the river Jordan preaching, 'Turn away from your sins and be baptised, and God will forgive your sins. As it is written in the book of the prophet Isaiah:

> Someone is shouting in the desert:
> "Get the road ready for the Lord,
> make a straight path for him to travel." '

In many different ways John preached the good news to the people and urged them to change their ways. *(Luke 3:3–4,18)*

Prayers for ourselves

God, we live in a world that needs to change. We are part of the world and we do things that hurt each other – things that are wrong.

Silence – to think about these things

We say to God:
GOD, WE ARE SORRY.
WE WANT TO BE DIFFERENT.
Listen to God's words, words for those who want to change.
In Jesus, God says to us:
Come with me, your sins are forgiven; don't be afraid, I love you.
GOD, THANK YOU.
THANK YOU FOR YOUR LOVE.

Prayers for others

We pray tonight for people whose ways are changing – for families where there is a new baby, for those who are ill, for those who have left home, for people in countries where wars and disasters are causing painful changes …

God, in your mercy,
HEAR OUR PRAYER.
AMEN

Song: Sing a song about change, about following Jesus (e.g. Lord of the dance; Sing hey for the carpenter; O Jesus, I have promised; Jesus' hands were kind hands)

Closing responses

As we plan and make decisions
GOD BE OUR WAY.
As we learn and ask questions
GOD BE OUR TRUTH.
As we grow and change
GOD BE OUR LIFE. AMEN

Discussion and activities: Talk about change. Before or during the liturgy, you could do some Advent cleaning – a cupboard, a room. Change five things in the room where you are meeting and then ask people to name them.

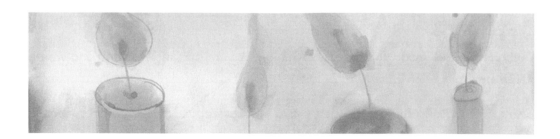

ADVENT THREE

Opening responses

When the world began
GOD SAID YES.
When Jesus came
GOD SAID YES.
When we were born
GOD SAID YES.
GOD SAID YES TO LIFE AND LOVING.

Bible reading

Reader: The psalmist reminds us that God made us and is always with us:

God, you created every part of me;
you put me together in my mother's womb.
When my bones were being formed,
when I was growing there in secret,
you knew that I was there;
you saw me before I was born.
God, where could I go to escape from you?
Where could I get away from your presence?
If I flew away beyond the East,
or lived in the farthest place in the West,
you would be there to lead me;
you would be there to help me.

(From Psalm 139)

Prayers

In our prayers we pray for those who travel:
We pray for people whose journeys are hard and dangerous.
We pray for people whose journeys are happy and hopeful.
We pray for people who make our journeys possible ...
We pray for ourselves, that we may be ready to go where God calls us.
God, in your mercy,

HEAR OUR PRAYER.
AMEN

Song: Sing a song about travelling (e.g. One more step; Jesus Christ is waiting; The wheels on the bus)

Closing responses

God calls us
TO ENJOY LIVING.
God calls us
TO BE LIKE JESUS.
God calls us
TO LIFE AND LOVING.
GOD, WHEN YOU CALL US, HELP US TO SAY YES.

Blessing

BLESS TO US, O GOD, THE ROAD THAT IS BEFORE US.
BLESS TO US, O GOD, THE FRIENDS WHO ARE AROUND US.
BLESS TO US, O GOD, YOUR LOVE WHICH IS WITHIN US.
BLESS TO US, O GOD, YOUR LIGHT WHICH LEADS US HOME. AMEN

Discussion and activities: Look at pictures/Christmas cards showing Mary and Joseph travelling. Talk about births in your family/community. Display childhood photographs of local adults; invite guesses.

ADVENT FOUR

Opening responses

Mountains and molehills
PRAISE GOD.
Puddles and seashores
PRAISE GOD.
Sweet-peas and stinging nettles
PRAISE GOD.
Elephants and money spiders
PRAISE GOD.
All of creation
PRAISE GOD.

Bible reading

Before the world was created the Word already existed; he was with God, and he was the same as God. From the very beginning, the Word was with God. Through him God made all things; not one thing in all creation was made without him. The Word was the source of life and this life brought light to humankind. The light shines in the darkness and the darkness has never put it out. (John 1:1–5)

Response to Bible reading:

In our watching and our waiting,
COME AMONG US, JESUS, BE OUR LIGHT.

Prayers

All over the world people wait for Jesus's birthday.
We remember people from many lands.

We pray for the people of ... (as you pray place candles on a map or beside a globe;
use visuals.)

God, in your mercy,
HEAR OUR PRAYER

Song: God's got the whole world in his/her hands

Closing responses

In our watching and our waiting
COME, LORD JESUS.
In our hopes and in our fears
COME, LORD JESUS.
In our homes and in our world
COME, LORD JESUS.
COME, BLESS US AND SURPRISE US,
AND HELP TO CELEBRATE YOUR BIRTHDAY. AMEN

Discussion and activities:

Research how people across the world prepare for and celebrate Christmas. Discover
some of their traditions; learn a Christmas song from another country (in another
language?).

Ask people to share with you how they celebrate Christmas.

Try out some food from another culture.

Ruth Burgess

(Advent is for everyone was originally written for, and distributed within, the Diocese of Ipswich.)

THE COMING KING
Meditative services for each week in Advent

For small groups

WEEK 1

The first candle

The first candle in the Advent circle is lit. (The Advent circle consists of four candles and a little greenery.)

1st voice:
We light the first candle of Advent
in the circle of God's eternity,
a circle green as the earth
where Jesus came to live with us.

Silence

2nd voice:
We light the first candle of Advent
to celebrate the prophets,
who waited long and looked with expectancy
for the coming of the Messiah

Silence

3rd voice:
We light the first candle of Advent for ourselves,
for we, too, wait with expectancy
for the coming of God's Kingdom
and the reign of Christ the King.

Silence

Reading

Romans 8:18–25 (All creation waits with expectant longing)

A question

What are your hopes – for yourself, your church, your country?

Prayer

Lord Christ, the prophets spoke of your coming
as a child to be born to a young woman.
In the pain and joy of children,
in the work and fellowship of homes,
YOUR KINGDOM COME.

Lord Christ, the prophets spoke of your coming
to bring justice, compassion and freedom.
In all just actions, compassionate acceptance
and desire for truth,
YOUR KINGDOM COME.

Lord Christ, the prophets looked for a renewed earth,
where desolation would be replaced by abundance.
In all active longing
to live in your world with love and gentleness,
YOUR KINGDOM COME.

Song

To - day, this ve - ry morn - ing, as a child, as a child, is ___ born the branch of Jes - se, as a child, The migh - ty one of Boz - rah, who ___ gave the law on Si - nai, who ___ made the peace on Cal - v'ry, is a child, is a child and ___ sucks the breast of Ma - ry, as a child.

Today, this very morning, as a child, as a child,
is born the branch of Jesse, as a child;
the mighty one of Bozrah,
who gave the law on Sinai,
who made the Peace on Calv'ry, is a child, is a child
and sucks the breast of Mary, as a child.

Ezekiel's living waters on her knee, Mary's knee;
see Daniel's true Messiah, on her knee;
Isaiah's child of wisdom,
the hope to Adam given,
the Alpha and Omega on her knee, Mary's knee,
is found in Bethl'hem's manger, on her knee.

Haste, sinner, now to meet him as you are, as you are;
as refuge sure, now greet him as you are;
the well of life has opened,

will cleanse and make the broken,
like Salmon's* snows, unbroken; therefore come, as you are,
to him whose grace is spoken, as you are.

From the Welsh of Daffydd Hughes (bardic name Eos Lal), translated by David Fox

*Psalm 68:14

Note: This is part of a plygain carol. The plygain tradition in rural north and mid-Wales stretches back over four centuries and is still vigorous in some areas. The plygain is a pre-dawn service held during Advent and Christmas time. It is a largely lay-led service, where groups sing carols extolling the birth, life and death of Jesus.

Prayer

Christ of the past and future,
stay with us now
and give us the courage
to search for your Kingdom. AMEN

WEEK 2

The second candle

Two candles in the Advent circle are lit.

1st voice:
We light the second candle of Advent
in the circle of God's eternity,
a circle green as the earth
where Jesus came to live with us.

Silence

2nd voice:
We light the second candle of Advent
to celebrate the young girl, Mary,
bearing the glory of the Godhead
to a waiting world.

Silence

3rd voice:
We light the second candle of Advent for ourselves,
for we, too, are given the task
to bear the light of Christ
into the dark places.

Silence

Reading

Luke 1:26–38 (Mary is visited by an angel)

A question

Mary is pictured in many ways on Christmas cards and in nativity plays. What words and pictures would you use to describe her?

Prayer

Lord Christ, born of Mary,
in our littleness,
in our weakness,
LET YOUR LIGHT SHINE.

Lord Christ, born of Mary,
in our strength
and our achievement,
LET YOUR KINGDOM COME.

Lord Christ, born of Mary,
in the overturning of our values,
in the renewing of your people,
LET YOUR KINGDOM COME.

Mary's song
(based on Luke 1:46–55)

With joy I lift my heart
to praise the greatness of the Lord,
my Saviour and my God.
With joy I sing his praise
because he has remembered me

in all my littleness.
All the world, in every time,
shall call me happy for this cause;
for my God has done great things,
my great God, holy is his name;
in every age he shows his love for those who honour him.

God has stretched out his arm
and all the proud with all their plans
are scattered far away.
Proud kings he has cast down
from off their thrones, while lifting up
the lowliest on earth.
Hungry he fills with good things;
the rich he sends empty away.
He has kept his promises
made to our people in the past,
to Abraham's descendants mercy for all times to come.

Mary's song
Codiad yr Ehedydd (The Rising of the Lark), traditional Welsh folk tune

Prayer

Christ, child of Mary,
come to us in joy and transformation;
let the brightness of your light shine. AMEN

WEEK 3

The third candle

Three candles in the Advent circle are lit.

1st voice:
We light the third candle of Advent
in the circle of God's eternity,
a circle green as the earth
where Jesus came to live with us.

Silence

2nd voice:
We light the third candle of Advent
to celebrate John the Baptist,
and all who point the way
to the coming Christ.

Silence

3rd voice:
We light the third candle of Advent for ourselves,
for we, too, are called
to prepare the way
for his coming.

Silence

Reading

Luke 3:1–20 (John's questions prepare us for Christ's Kingdom)

A question

What might John the Baptist say to us and to our nation today?

Prayer

With John the Baptist
and all your saints,
we ask this grace:

that we may know repentance for our sins
that is true and heartfelt;
let us prepare a way for the Lord
AND MAKE HIS PATHS STRAIGHT.

With John the Baptist
and all your saints,
we ask this grace:
that our nation may be turned around
to the values of God's Kingdom;
let us prepare a way for the Lord
AND MAKE HIS PATHS STRAIGHT.

With John the Baptist
and all your saints,
we ask this grace:
that your church may be renewed
by the fire of your Spirit;
let us prepare a way for the Lord
AND MAKE HIS PATHS STRAIGHT.

Song: Life is a journey

Ar Lan y Môr (Upon the shore), traditional Welsh folk tune

Life is a journey we are walking;
Sometimes it's hard, sometimes it's easy;
Sometimes we're puzzled and bewildered,
Walking onwards, walking onwards.

The way ahead is full of shadows;
We can't make sense of what is happening;
The world around full of confusion,
Walking onwards, walking onwards.

We need a light to cut through darkness;
We need a map to give direction;
We need a guide to walk beside us,
Walking onwards, walking onwards.

'I am the way,' God's son is saying.
'I'll light a pathway through the darkness;
I'll walk beside as your companion,
Walking onwards, walking onwards.'

Margaret Harvey

Prayer

Lord Christ, stay with us;
encircle us with your protection
as we walk on in the company of your saints
towards your Kingdom. AMEN

WEEK 4

The fourth candle

Four candles in the Advent circle are lit.

1st voice:
We light the fourth candle of Advent
in the circle of God's eternity,
a circle green as the earth
where Jesus came to live with us.

Silence

2nd voice:
We light the fourth candle of Advent
to celebrate the Christ who comes
as a babe at Bethlehem,
and in power and great glory at the end of time.

Silence

3rd voice:
We light the fourth candle of Advent for ourselves,
for we are called to be Christ's body
and to live in this time and place.

Silence

Reading

1 Corinthians 12:12–27 (All of you are part of Christ's body)

Question

How does being a member of the body of Christ affect your celebration of Christmas?

Prayer

Lord Christ, born in Bethlehem,
give us grace to live the generosity of your humility.
With great joy
WE CELEBRATE YOUR BIRTH.

Lord Christ, Lord of all creation,
give us grace to live the compassion of your justice.
With great joy
WE WAIT FOR YOUR COMING.

Lord Christ, whose Spirit is active
in your Church and your whole world,
give us grace to live the calling to be your body.
With great joy
WE PROCLAIM YOUR PRESENCE.

Song: Wondrous
(Tune: Esther or Hyfrydol)

Wondrous, wondrous to the angels,
wondrous to the saints of old,
that the God who made and rules us
and the whole creation holds
now lies swaddled in a manger,
born into our world of care,
yet a shining host in glory
bring him worship, bring him prayer.

Thousand, thousand thanks, and endless;
all my life shall sing the praise
of my God who for my worship
wondrous powers in manger lays.
Here in tempted human nature,
here – like weakest of our race,
here as helpless human infant,
here is God in power and grace.

From the Welsh of Ann Griffiths*, translated by David Fox

*(*Ann Griffiths lived in Montgomeryshire, in mid-Wales. She was born in 1776 and died at the birth of her first child in 1805. A farmer's wife, lacking formal education but with an intense experience of God, she is recognised as one of the great hymn writers of Wales.)*

Prayer

Lord Christ, stay with us
as we celebrate your coming
with joy and laughter
and with stillness and wonder. AMEN

Margaret Harvey

WAITING AND LONGING
A daily prayer practice for Advent

Introduction

During Advent we practise the discipline of opening our hearts to the presence of Christ in our midst; we wait for a glimpse of the truth that he is with us; we long to experience the joy of his presence and the wonder of the love of our God, who became flesh and dwelt amongst us and whose Spirit is with us, encouraging us to join in the living of God's Kingdom now.

Opening

Psalm 42:1 (sung or said):

Music: Annie Heppenstall-West

As a deer longs for flow-ing streams so my soul, so my soul, as a deer longs for flow-ing streams, so my soul longs for you O God.

Affirmation of faith in God's presence

The Psalmists prayed:
Deep calls to deep
at the thunder of your cataracts;
all your waves and your billows
have gone over me.
By day the Lord commands his steadfast love,
and at night his song is with me,
a prayer to the God of my life.
Psalm 42:7–8

You knit me together in my mother's womb. My frame was not hidden from you, when I was being made in secret, intricately woven in the depths of the earth …
Psalm 139:13–15

St Paul said:
In God we live and move and have our being.
Acts 17:28

I am convinced that neither death, nor life, nor angels, nor rulers, nor things present, nor things to come, nor powers, nor height, nor depth, nor anything else in all creation, will be able to separate us from the love of God in Christ Jesus our Lord.
Romans 8:38–39

Christ promised:
Remember I am with you always, to the end of the age.
Matthew 28:20

Light a candle and say: 'Christ is here.'

Pause

Meditating on scripture:

WEEK 1: Longing for the light of God's presence

Hosea 6:3

Let us press on to know the Lord;
his appearing is as sure as the dawn;
he will come to us like the showers,
like the spring rains that water the earth.

Meditation

As the sun is constant, so too is the love of God; it is we who, like the Earth, sometimes turn away and sometimes turn towards God. My waiting is for my own readiness to see the light.

Prayer

Light stirs through rain clouds.
I remember your deep love.
I long for your warmth.

Sunshine and rain

wake seeds deep within me.
I hunger for light.

Light of God, living water,
heal me, refresh me,
make me new.

Annie Heppenstall-West

WEEK 2: Longing for the lover of my soul

Song of Solomon 3:1b–4

I sought him, but found him not;
I called him, but he gave no answer.
I will rise now and go about the city,
in the streets and in the squares;
I will seek him whom my soul loves.
I sought him, but found him not.
The sentinels found me,
as they went about the city.
'Have you seen him whom my soul loves?'
Scarcely had I passed them,
when I found him whom my soul loves.

Meditation

My soul searches restlessly for the love of Christ, to know him and be one with him.

Prayer

I seek longingly,
in city streets and squares,
you, whom my soul loves.

As I search the streets
let me see you
in the eyes of the people there.

Let me find you
and bring you within my own house.
Let me hold you
my love, my dear one.

Annie Heppenstall-West

WEEK 3: Longing for that which is promised

Isaiah 42:6b–9

I have taken you by the hand and kept you;
I have given you as a covenant to the people,
a light to the nations,
to open the eyes that are blind,
to bring out the prisoners from the dungeon,
from the prison those who sit in darkness.
I am the Lord, that is my name;
my glory I give to no other,
nor my praise to idols.
See, the former things have come to pass,
and new things I now declare;
before they spring forth,
I tell you of them.

Meditation

It is the coming of the Kingdom of Shalom, the reign of the Prince of Peace, for which I long, on earth as in heaven.

Prayer

Hand in hand with God,
I will walk in light and justice.

Hand in hand with God,
I will be a light for others.

Hand in hand with God,
I will speak and live in love.

Annie Heppenstall-West

WEEK 4: Longing for the Christ Child

Luke 1:41–45

And Elizabeth was filled with the Holy Spirit and exclaimed with a loud cry, 'Blessed are you among women, and blessed is the fruit of your womb. And why has this happened to me, that the mother of my Lord comes to me? For as soon as I heard the sound of your greeting, the child in my womb leaped for joy. And blessed is she who believed that there would be a fulfilment of what was spoken to her by the Lord.'

Meditation

Fruit of the womb, the Human One, brother, friend, child, with a mother's longing to see her unborn, so I long to know you more deeply, my Christ.

Prayer

Grow in me, love-child.
Grow and fill me with life;
make me your home.

Grow in me, Christ-child;
be born of tears and pain
in unshakeable love.

Grow to fullness in me;
open me and live through me;
my body is yours.

Annie Heppenstall-West

Intercessions

Pray for those who need your prayers today.

Closing prayer

I pray
not only *Come, O Lord*,
but move me to let you in,
for already you stand at my door knocking,
your presence immediate, urgent, powerful;

not simply *be with me*, my God,
but let me feel your presence always,
for you are always here;

not so much *hear my prayer*,
but give me words which resonate
with the energy of your love,
for you are the eternal listener of our souls' song;

not always *help me*,
but let me learn to see your working in my life;

not *give me*,
but humble me,
that in my lowliness
I may fall no further;

not *protect me*,
but immerse me in life
and let me love and give and learn to follow
the driving, compelling power of your wild Spirit;

not *save me*,
but let me understand that
in the vastness of your universe
you lovingly surround me,
always and completely.
In you alone can I safely lose myself
and so find you.
Amen

Annie Heppenstall-West

Annie Heppenstall-West and Ray Gaston

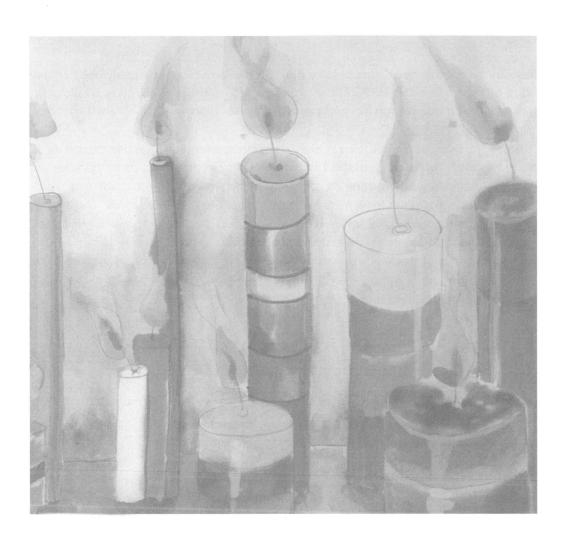

THE JESSE TREE

Jesse Trees

Jesse Trees show the genealogy of Jesus Christ in the form of a tree (family tree). Depictions of Jesse Trees can be found in stone carvings and stained glass windows in medieval and modern churches and cathedrals (Wells Cathedral, Dunblane Cathedral, Kilpeck Parish Church).

Jesse Trees can be created on a poster or a banner; alternatively, a branch or a small potted tree can be used. Symbols representing people or events (see opposite) are hung on the tree or stuck on the poster/banner. The symbols can be made from cardboard and painted, or cut from material, postcards or old Christmas cards. The process of designing and making the symbols gives adults and children an opportunity to talk together about the stories (choose stories that are familiar to children – Jonah and the whale, the creation story ...). Symbols can be created daily during Advent or at convenient times during the weeks of Advent. There are two genealogies of Jesus that you can refer to when making Jesse Trees: Matthew 1:1–17 and Luke 3:23–38.

A prayer for family use

Today we add _____ to our tree.
We thank you God for the family of Jesus.
We thank you for our family,
for _____ .
Please look after us all today. Amen

Ruth Burgess

Person/event	Symbol/s	Bible reference (by chapter)
Jesse Tree with branches		Isaiah 11
Creation	Stars and planets	Genesis 1
Adam and Eve	Fruit tree	Genesis 2
Noah and family	Ark/animals/dove/rainbow	Genesis 6–9
Abram and Sarah	Tent	Genesis 12
Jacob	Ladder	Genesis 28
Joseph	Multi-coloured coat	Genesis 37
Moses	Burning bush	Exodus 3
Miriam	Tambourine	Exodus 15
Aaron	Golden calf	Exodus 32
Rahab	Red cord	Joshua 2
Joshua	Trumpet	Joshua 6
Gideon	Water jar	Judges 7
Samson	Bees/scissors	Judges 14–17
Ruth	Ears of corn/sandal	Ruth 1–4
David	Harp	1 Samuel 16
Solomon	Temple	1 Kings 6
Elijah	Ravens	1 Kings 17
Nehemiah	Walls of Jerusalem	Nehemiah 1, 2
Isaiah	Flowers in the desert	Isaiah 35
Jeremiah	A well	Jeremiah 38
Daniel	Lions	Daniel 6
Jonah	Big fish/gourd/worm	Jonah 1–4
Habakkuk	Watchtower	Habakkuk 1–3
Zechariah	Old people/young children	Zechariah 8
Joseph	Saw/hammer	Matthew 1
Mary	A manger	Luke 1, 2

Jesse Tree song
(Tune: Dancing day)

God threw the planets into space
And angels danced on land and sea,
And Eve and Adam started the race
That found its end and beginning in me.

Chorus: Come sing and dance, come dance with me, with me, with me.
Come dance around the Jesse Tree.

Come matriarchs, prophets and righters of wrongs,
Come exiles and wanderers, slaves set free,
Come make glad music and sing wild songs
And dance around the Jesse Tree.

Chorus

Come buskers and bankers and scholars and kings,
Come pensioners, truck drivers, come, you and me,
Come bang the drum and let the bells ring
And dance around the Jesse Tree.

Chorus

Today and tomorrow we shall dance,
And stamp our feet and shout with glee.
With saints and angels hand in hand
We'll dance around the Jesse Tree.

Chorus

Ruth Burgess

LAST THINGS:
DEATH, JUDGEMENT
HEAVEN AND HELL

SHEEP

No free thinkers here.
We go with the flock,
never stick our scrag-ends out,
always do what's expected of us.
Who needs freedom
when we've this whole field to ourselves?
There's nothing out there
but wolves and rogue lambs
bleating on about
democracy and free speech,
not to mention vegetarianism.
Well, we don't care what anyone says,
one shepherd's much the same as any other
and they know what's best for us.

What's wrong with woolly thinking?
It keeps us snug and smug.
We know our place.
If we've done nothing wrong
we've nothing to worry about.
Right?

Nancy Somerville

I WALK DANGEROUS PATHS

I walk dangerous paths
the line
between right and wrong
I am not always right
(I am not always wrong)
no parallel lines
these
they
converge in places

where boundaries are not defined
and
I dream
of arrival

Liz Knowles

JESUS IS COMING
A play

Characters:
Narrator
Youths (Jo, Daz and Andy, Tina and Jan, Pete and Lee, Lara and Don)
Minister
Jesus

Narrator: It's almost two thousand years now since Jesus went home to his Father in heaven. But Jesus promised us that, one day, he'll come back. I wonder what people will be doing when he arrives …

(Jo, Daz and Andy run into the acting space.)

Jo: Spotty! Spotty! Andy's a spotty spaz!

Daz: Cry baby! Always running to teacher!

Andy: Leave me alone.

Jo: Let's push him in the mud.

Daz: Let's throw him in the nettles.

Andy: Stop it!

(Jo and Daz jump on Andy and start to thump him. Jesus comes in quietly and stands looking down at them.)

Daz: Here – who are you?

Jesus: I'm called Jesus.

Jo: You're dead.

Jesus: Do I look dead?

Andy: But nobody's seen you for hundreds of years.

Jesus: Haven't you been told? I promised I'd come back.

Jo: You're not really Jesus, are you?

Jesus: Oh yes ... yes, I am.

Daz: But if you're Jesus, and you have come back, then ...

Jesus: Well?

Daz: Then ... it's the end of the world?

Jesus: I'm afraid it is.

Jo: But ... then we ...

Jesus: Yes, you just spent the last ten minutes of your life behaving like a horrible bully. Andy – are you coming with me?

Andy: Yes please!

Daz: What about us?

Jesus: What do you think?

(*Andy stands beside Jesus. Daz exits. Tina and Jan come into the acting space.*)

Tina: Oh, do stop making such a fuss! I'm only taking a pound to buy pop.

Jan: But we raised that money for Children In Need!

Tina: Don't be stupid, it's only a pound. Everybody does it.

Jan: No, they don't.

Tina: Do stop whingeing. You don't have to have any pop if you don't want to. I'm thirsty.

Jan: I'm thirsty too, but that isn't our money. People gave it to us for Children In Need.

Tina: Yeah, yeah. Well, I'm a child, and I'm in need, so that's all right then, isn't it? Get out of my way.

(Tina pushes Jan. Jesus quietly catches her.)

Tina: What are you doing? You've been spying on us.

Jesus: Not really.

Jan: Who are you?

Jesus: I'm called Jesus.

Jan: And you've come back?

Jesus: Yes.

Jan: So, it's the end of the world?

Tina: It's the *what*?

Jesus: It's the end of the world.

Tina: Oh! So ...

Jesus: Yes, you just spent the last ten minutes of your life stealing money from a charity. Jan – are you coming with me?

Jan: Yes please!

Tina: What about me?

Jesus: What do you think?

          (Jan joins Jesus and Andy. Tina exits. Pete and Lee come into the acting space. They are balancing on something high up.)

Jesus: What are you doing, up there on the school roof?

Pete: We're allowed, so there!

Jesus: Are you?

Lee: Who are you?

Jesus: I'm called Jesus.

Lee: Oh no ...

Jesus: Yes, it's the end of the world, and you just spent the last ten minutes of your life doing something you've been told over and over again not to do.

Pete:	You're not going to ask us to come with you, are you?
Jesus:	What do you think?

(Pete and Lee exit. Lara and Don come into the acting space. They lie on the floor. Lara is drinking from a vodka bottle and Don is injecting something into his arm. Pete and Lee come rushing in.)

Pete:	Get up, quick!
Lara:	Woss matter?
Lee:	Jesus has come back; you mustn't let him catch you like this.

(Lara and Don try to get up. They fall over. Jesus comes over, looks at them sadly and goes out with Andy and Jan. The minister comes in and starts laying out a Bible, a cross and a candle. Pete and Lee struggle over to him supporting Lara between them, followed by Daz and Jo supporting Don, and Tina carrying her piggy bank.)

Minister:	What do *you* want?
Lee:	Let us in, quick! Jesus has come back.
Minister:	You can't come in here!
Pete:	We're allowed, so there!
Minister:	You most certainly are not allowed! We're just going to have a service. Look at those awful scruffy jeans. And I know what you've been doing. You two, Joseph and Daniel, you've been in trouble for bullying at every school governors' meeting this term. Peter and Lee, our community police officer has caught you in forbidden places at least once a week for the last five years. Christina – everybody knows what happens to the money you pretend to collect for charity. As for Lara, she's paralytic on vodka again, which is against the law as well as stupid; and I don't know what Donald has been taking, but it certainly isn't legal. Why should I let *you* in here?
Youths:	Because we're sorry!
Minister:	Sorry? I should think you are sorry. You've got a lot to be sorry for.
Tina:	So will you let us in, then?
Minister:	Certainly not!

(Jesus enters)

Jesus: How dare you!

Minister: I'm sorry? Who might *you* be?

Youths: He's Jesus!

Minister: Jesus? You've come back?

Jesus: As I promised.

Lee: Jesus, look, please, we're really sorry!

Jesus: Are you?

Youths: Yes!

Pete: Please forgive us.

Daz: It was mean of us to bully.

Jo: We've been thinking.

Tina: I've brought all my money, look. I want to pay back everything I took.

Tara: Jesus … help me …

Minister: Jesus, you're not going to fall for this, are you? They're just trying to get round you. They're not worth it.

Jesus: You snake. Be quiet. I never asked you to keep people *out* of my Father's house. *Not worth it?* These are my Father's dear children, and today they will be with me in Paradise. I died to let them be with me in Paradise.

Youths: Thank you, thank you.

Minister: Um … what about me?

Youths: What do you think?

Elizabeth Varley

WHAT WAS THE CATCH?

'Come on,' he said,
'there's lots of food, wine too,
and it's all waiting;
come and join the party, it'll be great.'

I hesitated.
I was hungry true enough,
and you have to take your chances when they come,
but it didn't feel right.
People just don't throw parties and then go out and look for guests.
It was all the wrong way round.
You have to be invited to a party.
And people usually only invite you if you can invite them back …
And I couldn't do that.

'Come on,' he said,
'it's only round the corner.
You'll make lots of friends,
and it's all free.
My master really wants you to come.

I stood and I looked at myself.
I wasn't dressed for a party.
I had no present to take.
And who was this master, this host?
I didn't even know his name.
And why did he want me at his party?
What was the catch?

Ruth Burgess

IF YOU CAME

If you came
with a fistful of anger,
who could endure?

But you come
with open hands,
eager to grasp our own in love.

If you came
with the fire of judgement,
who could endure?

But you come
with the light of grace
to show us the way.

If you came
hardened against our sin,
who could endure?

But you come
holding us in your heart,
that we might have life.

If you came
bearing bad news
we might be able to handle it.

But can we endure
the gift
of good news?

Even so,
come, Lord Jesus,
come.

Amen

Thom M Shuman

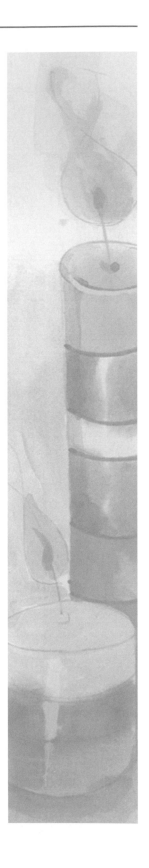

NO MESSING

No messing
Jesus
No messing

Love
Listen
Heal
Follow

No messing
No wriggling
No denial

I belong to you
and I must
say so
and live so.

So be it.
Amen

Ruth Burgess

GOD IS NOT LIKE THAT

I used to treat life as an exam,
a test you had to pass.
You know the sort of thing:
work hard, worry, try to guess
what the examiner wants.
Do your best, worry some more.
How silly can you get?

Life is not like that.
God (whatever the word means)
is not like that either.
Just being, just being human,
whatever it means,
is quite testing enough.

Frances Copsey

SITTING WITH MR FENTON
(From a longer story about working in a nursing home)

Mr Fenton's existence was limited to his bed – where he spent most of his time, bed rails up and locked like the sides of a crib during the hours no one was sitting with him – his washroom, and his desk where he sometimes, in slow motion, ate his meals.

Just getting Mr Fenton up for lunch was a miracle. We had to go in stages. And often, in the middle of operations, he would start to sway, about to collapse. I'd have to support him and be very careful setting him down as his bones were as brittle as dried out wood. When he did manage to make it to that other land that held his desk and red velvet chair, I'd arrange his tray for him and cut up any of his food that hadn't already been put through the blender. Though he'd often protest, I'd also straighten out the clutter on his table top, one of the places Mr Fenton was hoarding packets of fine cane sugar, salt and pepper, and little plastic tubs of real butter, blueberry jam, marmalade, and cream. I didn't see any point in throwing his mounting treasure out though, it would just upset him. Bolted to the back of his desk was a mirror. One morning I remember Mr Fenton peering into it and a look of shock breaking over his face. He probably hadn't been up for days and had forgotten what he looked like.

'I'm old ... I'm ugly ... I'm miserable ... I'm tired,' he croaked. Then, without swallowing a bite of sustenance, he motioned me to help him back to his bed, which I hadn't had a chance to change yet.

I was the sitter who changed the calendar the Royal Bank had sent him. It was eight months behind. I tried to do it as sensitively as possible. I didn't want to shock him. He became angry with me, and accused me of trying to trick an old man. Finally, he told me I could just go to hell. I scribbled in the Nurses' notes what had occurred, and that I thought Mr Fenton should be oriented to time and place every day now.

In these notes there were instructions for the sitter to get Mr Fenton up, to the shower, and dressed for the day. In the beginning, I attempted this routine.

'Stop trying to be Florence Nightingale,' Mr Fenton gargled, for the fourth time before I understood him. When he spoke it sounded like water going down a drain. In his pipes were clumps of phlegm. To understand him, I learned to offer him a sip of cool water through a striped straw between sentences and, later, between words.

I explained, somewhat frustrated, that I just wanted to give him a full life. He laughed at me. At first I thought he was choking. The way he was heaving for a moment I was afraid his joints might split.

'I haven't had one up till now,' he said in a gravelly voice, 'and it's not about to begin with you ... Come here, boy,' he said, motioning to me with a strictured hand. 'Look at me ... really look at me.'

I did finally.

'I'm waiting to die ... All right?'

I nodded.

I felt ashamed. He shouldn't have had to get my permission. From then on we got along. I stopped believing I knew better. I wasn't dying. When I sat with him, I'd get him what he asked for. 'Water.' And his drops. In the mornings, I'd first, with a warm face cloth, gently wipe the sand from the corners of his eyes. Standing over him with the eyedropper, his starved eyes straining wide, I felt like I was feeding a dying bird.

On Mr Fenton's desk was a gilt-framed photograph of the many-roomed house he had had to sell. I saw it made him happy, proud, to talk about it, so I'd say, 'That's a fine-looking house there, Mr Fenton. Just beautiful ...'

Mr Fenton died in a plush, sound-proofed room, leaving rumours of a great treasure buried in a bank vault somewhere; and, as if for banquets in the after world, a hoard of condiments to be excavated from secret compartments. From pockets in suit coats and from dresser drawers.

Neil Paynter

MY MOTHER WAS NOT MOST PLEASED

My mother
was not most pleased
that I, a schoolboy,
barely ten years old,
should be shown
my friend's dead aunt,
who lay at home in bed.

My first encounter
with the dead;
I sensed the need for quiet,
as children do,
and stood a while,
and tiptoed out again,
respectful, unperturbed.

Then or since,
I never knew why
my mother
was not most pleased,
for I had learnt
with gentleness
a fact of life.

Alan Horner

VICTORY

Brother death, I know you stalk me
at my shoulder night and day.
I do not fear thee, Christ is near me;
bright sword of Michael lights my way.
Through its light I will press onward
in the hope, the path, the way.

I feel no sadness, only gladness,
safe beneath God's covering wing;
brother death, get thee behind me,
I cannot feel thy awful sting;
night is passed and blessed morning
lifts me up, bird trumpets sing.

Brother death, you've lost the battle,
my God alone has won the day;
your darts of pain have torn and fraught me,
still my Saviour held the sway;
in his gentle arms he caught me;
bore me gently home to stay.

Davie Webster

DEATH IS A LONELY PLACE

death is a lonely place
where others cannot accompany you
even those of us that love you
can only come so far
and then look on

death is a lonely time
of remembering
when chance words and objects
bring back floods of memories
and tears

did I tell you I loved you?
did I ask you for all the answers you knew
and give you enough of me?

death is a lonely space
of emptiness
where you were once a presence
a brightness in our lives
and we are trying to get used to
missing you soon

this death is only you
and however much we love you
and pray for and think of you
it is only you
that can do it.

Liz Knowles
(For Patti Evans, my godmother, who died 20 August, 1994)

WAITING

Sometimes there are moments
when the world seems to stand still.

Moments which last for ever,
endlessly repeating,
like a stuck record.

The moment when the countdown ends,
before the mushroom blast
catapults us into a new and terrifying world.

The moment when the shot is fired,
before the President falls
and everything has changed.

The moment when we see the plane
and know that it will hit
and start the spiral into dark uncertainty.

The moment when the doctor says
that they can do no more
and we face another's death.

Will it be like that
when You return?
A moment of heart-stopping fear
before the Judgement
when You stand again
upon the Mount of Olives?

Or will it be the mingled joy and fear
when,
after the bloody battle of birth,
we wait, hushed,
for the newborn baby's cry?

Alix Brown

SEALING A COFFIN

Several years ago, an undertaker asked for a prayer that could be used for sealing a coffin. Kate McIlhagga wrote this prayer as a response to his request.

As I close the door on your earthly life,
may God open to you the gate of glory.

As your earthly life is sealed into death,
so may you rise with Christ.

May nails become
symbols of new life;
the wood that holds you,
symbol of salvation.

Kate McIlhagga

OVER

We walked in the graveyard.
The grave was open
waiting for the wooden box to come.
We snowballed each other to keep warm.
It was OK.
You would have laughed too.

And the cars came
and the flowers came
and the people.
And we laid you,
you and your ninety-three years of life,
in the earth.
And it was over.
And it was good.

Ruth Burgess

WATCHING & WAITING

ADVENT

Advent.
Once a year
the chance to wait
with a purpose.

Makes a change.

Carolyn Morris

ADVENT INTERCESSIONS

We are waiting, Jesus;
COME AND LIVE WITH US SOON.

Jesus, we are waiting because we know who you are:
the Creator of the world,
the God who took on human form,
the son of Mary, a girl just like any other girl.
We are waiting, Jesus;
COME AND LIVE WITH US SOON.

Jesus, we are waiting because we have faith in you.
We know that we can trust you.
We remember that you are good to us,
and we thank you for all the good things that you give to us every day.
We are waiting, Jesus;
COME AND LIVE WITH US SOON.

Jesus, we are waiting here,
here in Wavertree*, here in Liverpool*,
waiting for you to come into our houses, our streets, our shops and offices, to fill them
with your light and peace.
We are waiting, Jesus;
COME AND LIVE WITH US SOON.

Jesus, we are waiting for you to come and change things:
to bring health to our sick ones,
to make our asylum seekers welcome,
to comfort those who have lost loved ones;
and to turn us around

so that we can be your hands and feet,
your ears and eyes,
in this world that needs you so much.
We are waiting, Jesus;
COME AND LIVE WITH US SOON. AMEN

John Davies

*Substitute local place names

IN OUR WAITING

God, we come to you in our waiting.

We wait with our fears,
our anxieties and frustrations,
our pains and regrets,
our shame and confusion.
God, help us to wait in peace.

Pause

We wait with impatience:
We rush around, preparing for the festivities,
not leaving the space to prepare
our hearts.
God, help us to wait in faith.

Pause

We wait in excitement:
We are ready to celebrate!
We know the story with its humbleness, simplicity,
and wonder.
God, help us to nurture our joy.

Pause

We wait in thanksgiving:
We are free and able to celebrate.
We have others around us to share in the journey.
We are able to wonder in the marvel of your gift.
God, help us to receive your love. AMEN

Katrina Crosby

ADVENT IN TAMIL NADU, SOUTH INDIA

The following material was inspired by a three-month stay at a theological college in Madurai, Tamil Nadu State, South India.

Prayers for Advent

In the Tiruneveli area[1], crops lie under flood water, putting farmers under pressure. We pray especially for all people involved in growing, nurturing and harvesting the food we eat daily. Yet as we eat, many go starving …

WE ARE WAITING, WE ARE LOSING PATIENCE WAITING FOR ALL TO HAVE FOOD.

For the reconciliation which occurred between one family and twenty-four other families in Ramankulam[2], we give thanks. Yet too many painful divisions and barriers remain in India. We pray for these divisions and barriers to be broken down and healed …

WE ARE WAITING, WE ARE LOSING PATIENCE WAITING FOR RECONCILIATION TO BEGIN.

In Kodaikanal, bonded slave labour was ended. We pray for those in need of justice and those who pursue justice …

WE ARE WAITING, WE ARE LOSING PATIENCE FOR INJUSTICE TO END.

We pray for people in countries where Advent has become commercialised and falsely festive, empty of the true, simple and profound message of Christmas. We pray that you will help all people who have lost the way …

WE ARE WAITING, WE ARE LOSING PATIENCE WAITING FOR A RETURN TO THE REAL CHRISTMAS MESSAGE.

We pray for Joseph John[3] and his hopes and dreams of Indianised worship. For his legacy of Indian-style churches, and for their striking simplicity and beauty, we give thanks. We pray for worship and worship space to be enriched by Indian culture …

WE ARE WAITING, WE ARE LOSING PATIENCE WAITING FOR DIFFERENCE TO BE VALUED.

We pray that the hope of 'oru olai'[4] will become a reality on earth. We pray that food will be shared. We pray for oppressors to be liberated from their destructive ways.

WE ARE WAITING, WE ARE LOSING PATIENCE WAITING FOR OPPRESSION TO END.

HELP US TO LIVE OUR FAITH BY PURSUING JUSTICE,
BEING KIND
AND WALKING HUMBLY WITH YOU, GOD,
NOW AND FOR EVER. AMEN

Notes:

1 Tamil Nadu had not had rainfall at the monsoon season for three years from 2001-2004. Ironically, after drought, this caused flooding in some areas.
2 This refers to a dispute over access to land.
3 Joseph John was a Dalit who chose to give up being a pastor in order to live alongside village people. He worked to find ways of meaningfully weaving the Bible into daily life.
4 The Tamil words 'oru olai' mean 'one pot'. Poor people's food in South India is watered-down rice gruel.

Advent in Tamil Nadu

No brightly coloured lights
no tinsel
no mad shopping rush.

For today is today.

There may not be work in the fields
and the family need food, clothes, shelter.

Waiting ...

for hearts and minds
to open up
to Jesus Christ

and the possibilities
this unfolds for
our today and our tomorrow.

Another waiting at Kanniyakumari*

Unforgettable images:
fishermen in a huddle mending nets;
boats, all brightly coloured, nestling on sand;
goats dancing on a wall;

soap suds in the street as women wash clothes;
traders shouting out from market stalls;
rickshaw hooters incessant;
and people,
a sea of people,
waiting to go to the offshore temples.

People everywhere –
men, women and children.

To this hustle and hub of life
the tsunami came,
and so people are
waiting for life to return to normal,
waiting for life to begin again,
waiting for ...
waiting for ...

* Kanniyakumari is located at the southern tip of India where the Indian Ocean, Arabian Sea and Bay of Bengal meet. It is a significant place of pilgrimage for Hindus, who visit two offshore temples; the temples are built upon rocks jutting out of the sea.

An Advent service not to forget

Each year the Tamil Nadu Theological Seminary has an Advent service. Blue lights are hung from the trees lining the long, narrow avenue to the college and lots of lanterns are wired to the electricity cable. Each year the college chooses a theme; for 2004–2005 it was 'Towards the fullness of life'.

The air is pregnant with joy
and excited anticipation.
Storm clouds gather;
monsoon rain gushes and splutters,
but spirits cannot, will not, be dampened.

Come, come, *
for this is the time
to celebrate Advent.

Handmade lanterns glow with the message
'Towards the fullness of life'.
There is a multi-coloured fish,
a yellow globe surrounded by men and women holding hands,
a broken terracotta pot containing the word *Justice* ...

Come, come,
for this is the time
to celebrate Advent.

Tamil songs
leave lingering messages on the night air:
Amidst suffering
there is hope –
we are waiting
for Jesus to be born.

Come, come,
for this is the time
to celebrate Advent.

*'Come, come' is a phrase spoken regularly by Tamils to visitors.

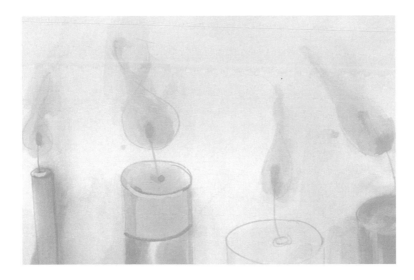

This is some Advent

Waiting for what?
For all to have clean drinking water.

Waiting for what?
For all to have food.

Waiting for what?
For women to be treated equally to men.

Waiting for what?
For workers to receive a fair wage.

Waiting for what?
For the rich to share their wealth.

Waiting for what?
For the caste system to end.

Waiting for what?
For baby Jesus to be born.

This is some Advent.

Waiting for rather a lot
it seems …

Rosie G Morton

GOD OF WAITING

God of birth,
we watch in fear for your coming;
scared of the pain and risk,
the struggle of new life emerging
and our own capacity to bear it.
God of waiting,
WAIT WITH US.

God of the future,
we watch in hope for your coming;
anticipating an unknown future,
uncertain of the unnamed reality,
not sure of the form it will take.
God of waiting,
WAIT WITH US.

God of celebration,
we watch in joy for your coming;
expectant with promises of freedom,
eager for new possibilities,
delighting in the gift of birth.
God of waiting,
WAIT WITH US.

Jan Berry

MAYBE

Maybe it is in the waiting for God,
not in the wandering from store to store,
that we find our way.

Maybe it is in the friendship of God,
not in the frenzy of the crowds,
that we are led to the manger.

May it is in the steadfast love of God,
and not in the pile of stuff under the tree,
that we find what we have been searching for all our lives.

Maybe, just maybe, God of Advent,
this year will be different.

Maybe, just maybe,
we will let you lead us to Bethlehem.

Thom M Shuman

GOD WAITS

God waits silently
in our inner recesses,
the chambers of our soul,
gazing lovingly
on our treasure,
awaiting our response.

Yvonne Morland

WAITING

Waiting.
To be free of this overcrowded space
and the permanent stench of ammonia.
Waiting to be packed into a crate,
and slaughtered by a machine.
To be plucked, eviscerated,
and pumped full of water.
Not plump enough.
Waiting for the holocaust:
Father, come and carve the roast.

Waiting.
Marking the days with steady breath,
my lungs swaying in the breeze.
Waiting, planted too densely,
to be cut, and gasp my last
in some stuffy living room,
choked with trinkets and fake snow.
Not beautiful enough.
Waiting to grow cones.
Son, come help us dress the tree.

Waiting.
For a life I can afford,
for economic freedom.
Waiting, in a crowded, noisy workplace,
assembling foreigners' gifts,
my fingers strained with repetition.
Not fast enough.
Waiting for the end of my shift.
Come Holy Ghost of Christmas presents.

Waiting.
For jingle bells all the way,
the malls bedecked with boughs of holly.
Waiting for a very merry Christmas,
everybody having fun,
mistletoe and wine.
It's only September.
Not soon enough –
I can't wait!

Gary Polhill

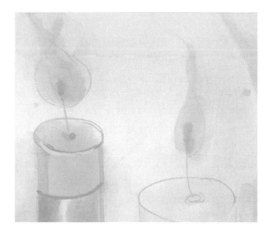

BE STRONG, TAKE HEART

Voice 1:   Wait on the Lord.
ALL: BE STRONG, TAKE HEART AND WAIT FOR THE LORD. *(Psalm 27:14)*

Voice 2:   For those who wait in queues at immigration control centres,
at factory or farm gates or employment agencies.
Voice 3:   'Will we be turned away again today?'
ALL: BE STRONG, TAKE HEART AND WAIT FOR THE LORD.

Voice 2:   For those who live in crowded, damp accommodation in former hospitals
or schools or old hotels, dependent on a politician's whim.
Voice 3:   'Can we ever make a home again?'
ALL: BE STRONG, TAKE HEART AND WAIT FOR THE LORD.

Voice 2:   For those who fear the onset of each night – a police raid, the destruction
of their tents, another rape, the kidnap of a child ...
Voice 3:   'O God, what madness drives our fate?'
ALL: BE STRONG, TAKE HEART AND WAIT FOR THE LORD.

Voice 2:   For those who know their sickness has no cure,
and that drugs that might prolong their lives are out of reach.
For children already fatherless, who are asked to watch and care.
Voice 3:   'O Lord, I have not deserved this.'
ALL: BE STRONG, TAKE HEART AND WAIT FOR THE LORD.

Voice 1:   For those who campaign courageously for justice,
who distribute food in spite of gunfire,
who work in crowded health clinics ...

Voice 2:   For those who must walk four miles a day carrying water,
who strive to create a future for their community's children.

Voice 3:   Listen to the words of Jesus:

Will not God judge in favour of his own people who cry out to him day
and night for help? Will he be slow to help them? I tell you, he will judge
in their favour and do it quickly. But will the Son of Man find faith on
earth when he comes? *(Luke 18:7)*
ALL: BE STRONG, TAKE HEART AND WAIT FOR THE LORD. AMEN

Liz Gregory-Smith

LIGHT AND DARKNESS

LIGHT AND DARKNESS: FROM A SERMON

Be on the alert and pray always, that you will have the strength to go safely through all those things that will happen, and to stand before the Son of Man.
Luke 21:36

I'd like to begin by quoting Richard Horsley, a biblical scholar from the United States. Horsley writes: *Imagine a complex, multi-cultural society that annually holds an elaborate winter festival, one that lasts not simply a few days, but several weeks. This great festival celebrates the birth of the lord and saviour of the world, the prince of peace, a man who is divine. People mark the festival with great abundance – feasting, drinking, gift-giving. Public space is festooned with images and decorations of the season. Special public events – song, dance, theatre, sporting events – happen almost daily. Local political and religious leaders preside over various rituals and cere-monies. The economy booms. The sales of goods and services flourish as at no other time of the year. The poor are recipients of special philanthropy and generous giving by the rich. In all, a great festival, which brings a sense of civic unity while honouring the saviour.*

Is Horsley talking about the contemporary experience of Christmas? Not at all. He is describing a major festival of the Roman Empire – the festival of celebration of the Emperor's divinity. This was celebrated at the time of Jesus's birth and throughout the early Christian period. This was the world that Jesus was born into and in which the early Church grew. A world in which the Emperor was called 'the lord and saviour of the world', 'the prince of peace' (the same images spoken by the angels at Jesus's birth). This says something very important: It says that, through the birth of Jesus Christ, God was offering the world a very different Saviour. Horsley makes it clear that the early Christians were being asked an all-important question: Who is your Saviour? The Emperor or Jesus Christ?

And so what is the question that the stories of the birth of Jesus raise for us today? As we start Advent and begin the Christian new year, what else is starting around us? If I could take you into the centre of Leeds, the city where I live, you'd see the 'Christmas' lights are up, people are out shopping late; an advertising hording proclaims 'Keep The Spirit Of Christmas Alive After Five'. The pilgrimage to the shopping centres is under way, and if you were shopping in Leeds city centre you would inevitably end up in THE LIGHT. That's right, a place called THE LIGHT! It's just amazing; it's a temple to consumerism. And if you were, instead, to take a trip down the motorway to one of the great out-of-town shopping centres, you'd enter what can only be described, both architecturally and metaphorically, as cathedrals of shopping. They cry out: Come and worship at this temple! This is The Light. Come and shop. This is where you get the light from. This is where the truth is. Worship the god of the free market. The god of the free market wants you to spend your money. And the god of the free market can give you money – why don't you take out a loan? Buy all those things you want. Let me give you what you want, what you think you need, what I tell you you need. And this is what you need: consumer goods. It doesn't matter if you haven't got any money at the moment; tell you what, you can 'buy now, pay later'.

And, by God, will you pay! Whether it's an official scheme of a major chain store or a loan shark preying on the poor, you will pay. People are dragged into traps in which they become possessed by debt. We have to ask ourselves why it is that people earning £50,000 a year and more are in massive amounts of debt. What's going on in our world? This Christmas there will apparently be £12 billion of credit card debt in the UK.

Bah humbug! You're just an old Scrooge, I hear you say. You don't want anybody to enjoy themselves. But that's not what it's about. It's about real enjoyment. Not this kind of manufactured enjoyment, not this kind of created need the god of the free market wants to drag us into. And so, as we walk into this winter festival of consumerism – or Consumermas, as I call it – we need to challenge it by really getting into Advent. And this isn't a Sunday extra option; this is about actually taking it on. Advent helps us to take on consumerism. Advent was set up to challenge the mid-winter Roman festival with all its over-indulgence and excess and celebration of the Emperor. It was actually set up to do that. So, just as Advent was a challenge to the Roman worship of the Emperor, it can be a challenge to our culture's worship of consumerism and the god of the free market.

Advent is a time for us not to zoom down to The Light, but to be still and get into the darkness. A time to discover God's presence in the darkness. A time of quiet. A time when instant gratification – buy now, pay later – is not on the agenda. Instead, what is on the agenda is waiting. And what we wait for is, in fact, a free gift. What we wait for is the Christ child, who is given to us absolutely free. What we wait for is an experience of God's grace, which is given to us absolutely free. No interest. Free. Absolutely free.

We wait in the darkness. We wait in the darkness of our season, the God-given seasonal spread. We notice the nights drawing in. We find spaces to actually notice that darkness (rather than the LIGHTS of the city centre). And we notice the darkness of our world – the violence and pain; and we open our hearts to that darkness. We notice the darkness in our own lives, our personal struggles. And in noticing that darkness we may experience a sense of the absence of God; but we know – from experience, from our stories, from tradition, from liturgy – that, as the psalmist says, 'Even the darkness is not dark to you, for the night is as bright as the day, for darkness is as light to you.' We know that in the darkness, in all those places of darkness, God is still present, already present, that Christ is with us in our struggles, even though we may not feel him there.

So, in the darkness we wait for the coming of the Light into the world.

This coming is seen as something in the future, but, actually, it's about presence, it's about being able to touch the reality of God's presence in the here and now. And the way we do that is by being alert! And how are we to be alert? We are to be alert, as the gospel says, by actually walking the path; we are to be alert by taking the opportunity of times like Advent to open our hearts more fully to God and Christ; to resist being dragged into consumerism and the way we are told we should be living our lives. We wait on the coming of the Light into the world by disciplining ourselves, by living that wait through our liturgy, our worship, our prayer-life – by using this time of Advent to practise that sense that we need to have all the time. That understanding that, if we're seriously going to be Christian resisters – resisters of the violence and the hatred in the world, proclaimers of love – then we're on a life-long journey. Advent is a time to practise the discipline of being, what Dorothee Solle called patient revolutionaries. Patient revolutionaries – always there ready to resist the unjust powers, in a way that actually proclaims Christ. Resistance through challenge and love. Patient revolutionaries – living that resistance by expressing the hope of Christ …

Christ is with us at this time of Advent, in the darkness, and Christ is coming with his Light – not the light of the shopping centre, but the Light of love and truth and beauty …

Ray Gaston

A CALL TO WORSHIP

Let us prepare to welcome our God!

A distant star glinting in the indigo sky:
COME, JESUS, COME.

A blazing beacon lighting up the way:
COME, JESUS, COME.

An energising sun brightening a gloomy day:
COME, JESUS, COME.

(Advent candle(s) may be lit.)

Judith Jessop, Broomhill Methodist Church

DECLARATION

We await the Christ,
THE ONE WHO WILL REVEAL GOD TO US.
He comes to us as sparkling light:
TWINKLING WITH JOY AND PLAYFULNESS.
He comes to us as everyday light:
BRIGHTENING THE ORDINARY WORLD AROUND US.
He comes to us as softened light:
CREATING A GENTLE, HEALING SPACE IN THE SHADOWS.
He comes to us as a focused spotlight:
BRINGING TRUTH AND JUSTICE INTO STARK RELIEF.
This is the Light of the world –
JESUS CHRIST, COMING TO SHINE AMONG US.

Judith Jessop, Broomhill Methodist Church

WE SEE THE LIGHT

In violent times,
beautiful words,
centuries old,
resonant with truth:

'Because of your light, Lord,
we see the light.'*

That light, even now,
illumining
our terror-stricken age
with the possibility of change:
offering our over-burdened hearts
a resting place
that a deeper compassion
may be our companion –

an energy of love
to struggle for justice,
to be a wounded healer,

to share what we have,
to carry hope in our hearts,
to laugh and to love,
perhaps, all in one day!

Peter Millar

Psalm 36:9

GOD, WAKE US UP

God of new creation,
when we are sleeping,
exhausted by activity
and the demands upon us:
WAKE US WITH A BURST OF LIGHT
TO LEAD US WITH JOY INTO YOUR DAY.

God of the unexpected,
when we are sleeping,
dulled by apathy
and indifferent to the needs around us:
WAKE US WITH A BURST OF LIGHT
TO LEAD US WITH JOY INTO YOUR DAY.

God of judgement,
when we are sleeping,
hiding from the truth
and shutting out the pain of reality:
WAKE US WITH A BURST OF LIGHT
TO LEAD US WITH JOY INTO YOUR DAY.

God of all life,
wake us up!
Re-create us,
surprise us,
challenge us,
that we may be ready to greet your light
and walk with joy through the day.

Jan Berry

BRIGHT GOD OF ADVENT

Bright God of Advent:
Blaze in our darkness.
Incinerate our iniquity.
Light up our road.

Riddle the ashes
of our desires.
Rekindle in us
your justice and love.

Ruth Burgess

A PENITENTIAL LITURGY FOR ADVENT

Reader: We live in a world oppressed by sin,
          a world of hunger, pain, injustice.
ALL: WE ACKNOWLEDGE THAT WE ARE PART OF THIS WORLD
          AND HAVE NOT ALWAYS PLAYED OUR PART
          IN CONFRONTING THE DARKNESS
          AND BRINGING THE LIGHT OF CHRIST TO TROUBLED PLACES.

Reader: We are part of the Body of Christ,
          a Body which is broken by the sin of its members.
ALL: WE RECOGNISE THAT WE BELONG TO THE BROKEN BODY OF CHRIST.
          THAT OUR LIVES ARE TOUCHED BY THE SIN OF OTHERS
          AND THAT OUR SIN TOUCHES THEIR LIVES.

Reader: We are unique individuals
          created in the image and likeness of God.
ALL: WE CONFESS THAT WE DO NOT LIVE UP TO GOD'S DREAM FOR US:
          THAT WHERE GOD SAYS: 'LET THERE BE LIGHT!',
          WE FEAR TO COME OUT OF THE SHADOWS;
          WHERE GOD SAYS: 'YOU ARE SALT FOR THE EARTH',
          WE REST CONTENT WITH BLANDNESS;
          WHERE GOD SAYS: 'BEFORE I FORMED YOU IN THE WOMB I KNEW YOU',
          WE LIVE ESTRANGED FROM HIM,
          AFRAID OF THE POWER OF GOD'S LOVE FOR US.

Scripture reading (Isaiah 40:15 or John 3:16–21)

An opportunity for individual or general confession and absolution
(This could include a symbolic action – e.g. lighting candles beside an empty crib.)

Closing responses

Reader: We gathered as people aware of the shadow that sin casts upon the world.
ALL: WE PART AS PEOPLE WHO HAVE CELEBRATED
              THE HEALING LOVE OF GOD:
              GOD'S POWER TO DISPEL THE DARKNESS
              OF OUR HEARTS AND MINDS AND SOULS.

Reader: And so may the God of tenderness and compassion,
              who entered this world so weak and so vulnerable,
              bless us today and every day unto eternity;
ALL: THE MAKER, THE HEALER, THE HOLY SPIRIT.

Reader: And until we meet again
ALL: MAY GOD HOLD US IN THE PALM OF HIS HAND.
              AMEN

From Wellspring

CARRYING A CANDLE

Carrying a candle
from one little place of shelter
to another
is an act of love.

To move through the huge
and hungry darkness, step by step,
against the invisible wind
that blows for ever around the world,
carrying a candle,
is an act of foolhardy hope.

Surely it will be blown out:
the wind is contemptuous,

the darkness cannot comprehend it.
How much light can this tiny flame shed
on all the great issues of the day?
It is as helpless as a newborn child.

Look how the human hand,
that cradles it, has become translucent:
fragile and beautiful; foolish and loving.
Step by step.

The wind is stronger than this hand,
and the darkness infinite
around this tiny here-and-now flame
that wavers, but keeps burning:
carried with such care
through an uncaring world
from one little place of shelter to another.
An act of love.

The light shines in the darkness
and the darkness can never put it out.

Jan Sutch Pickard

RE-ENCHANTED

Within these fragmented days,
a gentle invitation
threads through our lives,
reminding us that all is sacred
and rooted
in a love that knows no bounds

And with that quiet knowledge we re-enchant our times,
taking risks on holy ground:
hearing God's heartbeat in our global discomfort,
halting our harshness in our work for justice,
loosening our souls as our fears are named,
recognising new markers
in the passions of our prayers.

Re-enchanted,
we journey freely,
re-imagining God's presence
with re-awakened minds;
discovering afresh that surprising healing Word
which today, so powerfully,
illumines our poverty of understanding.

Peter Millar

DARKNESS AND LIGHT
A creed for Advent

We believe in God,
robed in splendour,
veiled in mystery,
ruler alike of darkness and light.

We encounter God
in Jesus Christ,
who was tortured and put to death,
but whose radiance could not be quenched;
whose touch brings a blaze of colour
to a dull, drab world:
reviving the weary,
healing the wounded,
dazzling the satisfied.

We walk with God,
guided by the light of God's loving spirit,
who enters the shadowed places of our hearts
and leads us into truth and life.

We wait for God,
and for the fulfilment of God's promises,
for the time when the darkness will hold no fear
and the light will no longer blind,
but creation will be made whole once more
and God's peace will reign for ever.
Amen

Cally Booker

IN THE DARK WITH JESUS

In the dark with Jesus,
held in tenderness,
silent, simply waiting,
deepest rest.

In the dark with Jesus,
quiet, hidden growing,
inner rubbish sorting,
frenzy stilled.

God's glory wrapped in shadows;
brightness hid for love's sake.
Contentedly beside us
when life's light is blinding.
For in the dark with Jesus,
healing comes.

Chris Polhill

CHRISTMAS TREE

Words and music by Pat Livingstone

Note: I built this piece of music starting with just the ostinato and then the ostinato and melody, then the ostinato plus the second part, etc. Build it up however you like.

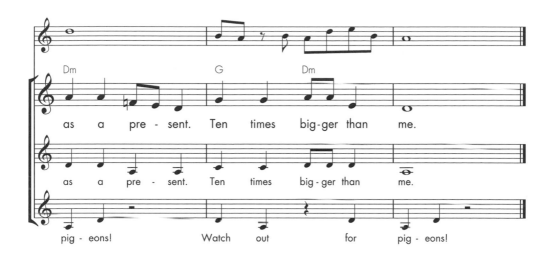

Performance note

This and the following two pieces are part of a longer work entitled 'Winter Lights', which was written for young people. It was originally intended as a flexibly scored work with additional parts for four adult musicians. These extracts are also intended to be played with whatever instrumentalists or singers are available. The material can be used in a flexible way by playing line by line and mixing them to make a longer piece. This was how the work was conceived.

Pat Livingstone

CHRISTMAS SHOPPING

Words and music by Pat Livingstone

Christ-mas shop-ping is good fun, buy-ing gifts for ev-ery-one.

Look, the lights are glow - ing. It has start-ed snow - ing.

2. I have bought a tie for dad.
    Hanky for gran who's sad.
    Plastic doll for Julie.
    Sweets for little Judy.

3. Nearly time to make for home.
    Got my bag, my purse, my comb.
    Look the bus is coming.
    People starting running.

THE LIGHTS

Words and music by Pat Livingstone

Note: Rondo. This piece follows the pattern ABACA.

I love to see the lights shi - ning, shi - ning bright - ly.

I love, I love to see the lights shi - ning bright - ly.

Bright - 'ning, cheer - ing the dark nights.

Glow - ing soft - ly in the trees. Bright - 'ning, cheer - ing

the dark nights. Glow - ing soft - ly.

now play A again

Watch the work - ers climb the trees. Tie the lights and scrape their knees.

Watch them ban - ish night with the hang - ing lights.

now play A again

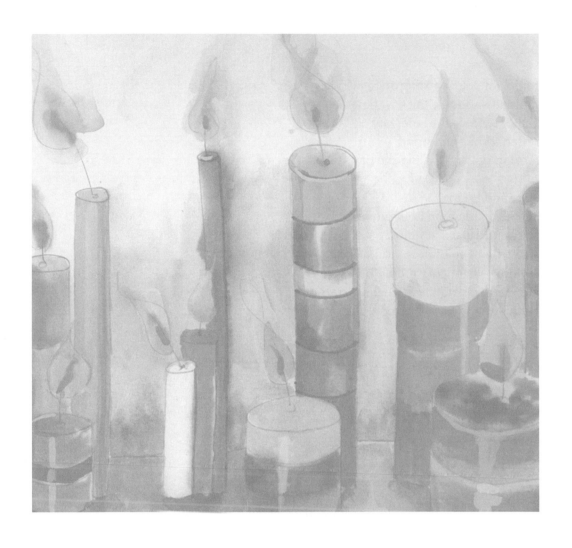

JOURNEYING
THROUGH ADVENT

STARS

Midnight cold – a Shropshire hillside,
footpaths sodden, thick with mud.
Ten of us from the inner city
rested awhile and stood,
looking up, and tracing the pattern
of stars in a night sky,
clear and bright,
aching a little from bodies unused
to country walks at night.
And a boy's voice broke the silence
saying, 'Where are we going then –
are we following these bleeding stars
all the way to Bethlehem?'

Ruth Burgess

GOD OF THE STREETS

God of the streets,
of our own street,
of every street;
comforting us in the pain that living brings,
celebrating with us our times of joy and exhilaration,
confronting us in our confusion and in our certainty.

God of the streets,
of our own street,
of every street,

walk with us through this Advent time,
in every street,
in every town. Amen

James Curry

OPENING PRAYER

God of the cosmos, God of the humdrum,
be with us today:
share our gladness at our meeting,
inspire our talking and listening,
enjoy our laughter and vision,
and be glorified in the 'someone has to do it' chores.
May your irrepressible adventurous Spirit be in us
today and every day,
as we journey towards
all that you call us to be. Amen

Frances Copsey

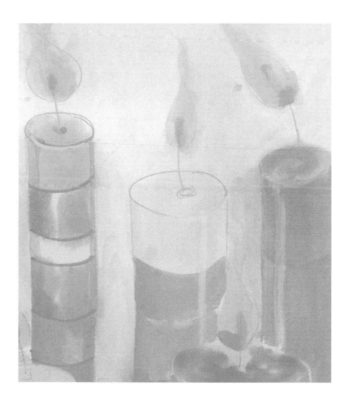

EVERY EVENING

Every evening
it's the same:
put the key in the deadbolt,
turn and lock;
check the windows;
put out the cat;
leave a light on …

All those routines
to feel safe
and fall asleep in peace.

But some night,
in the midst of my security,
you will tiptoe into my house,

rearranging the furniture,
cracking the combination
of my heart,
and ransacking
all my fears;

then,
softly whistling
Come, Thou Long-Expected Jesus,
you will slip out,
leaving the door
standing
wide open

that I might
follow you
into the kingdom.

Come, Lord Jesus!
Amen

Thom M Shuman

ADVENT ADVENTURE

Adventure is scary and exciting,
a journey into the unknown.
What dangers, what discoveries await us,
wrapped in the folds of the future,
we do not know.
This Advent adventure is different.
Something comes towards us
through the darkness;
our candles are tokens
of unimaginable light.

Frances Copsey

VERY SHORT ADVENT CONFESSION

Creator of light and darkness,
we so often chase shadows
and fail to walk in the light.

Forgive us, O God.

A time of stillness

We travel through Advent
as forgiven people,
lifting our faces towards the light.
Let us walk together
in hope and in faith.

Amen

Alison Adam

BRIGHT STAR-MAKER GOD

Bright star-maker God,
travel with us
through Advent

shine into our
dark corners

lead us into
ways of justice

warm us
with joy and wonder

bring us
to new birth.

Ruth Burgess

WE STAND AMAZED

Lord God, what a risk there was in your becoming flesh!
What a depth of self-giving love for your world!

We stand amazed
at such power bent by such love
to accept such humiliation
for such as us.

We stand amazed
that suffering love
should be the power above all power,
the power which transforms the universe
and wins its freedom.

We bless and adore our incredible Lord;
God most high brought low for our sakes.

Ian M Fraser

SEND US OUT WITH ANTICIPATION AND JOY

At this time of Advent,
fire our imaginations
with the sweep of your salvation.

Catch us up
in the cause of your kingdom,
already breaking into this world
in our ransomed lives
yet waiting for its final fulfilment when Christ shall come again.

And let your Spirit,
wild as the wind,
gentle as the dove,
move within us and among us,
to enliven our worship and strengthen our faith
and send us out with anticipation and joy.

John Harvey

ADVENT APPROACH

God of time and space,
we are glad to be here
on this Advent night.
For in your company we belong,
and this is a great mystery.

King of kings,
we dimly understand your power.
Light of life,
we cannot hide from you.
Saviour of the poor,
we bear witness to your compassion.
Word of truth,
we submit to your wisdom.
Flesh of our flesh,
we know we are understood by you.

We, who so carelessly forget your will
in our daily lives.
We, whose hearts are so often
filled with the wrong things.
We, who so typically squeeze every minute
out of these days
to get the last present bought,
the last call made,
the preparations finalised.

But this time is for you
and so let us stop.
Let us still our buzzing heads,
relax our weary bodies
and breathe deeply with your breath.

Pause

In this moment,
in this welcoming stillness,
we acknowledge our need of your waiting time.
And we ask your forgiveness
on all our lack of care –

for you,
for ourselves,
and for others –
in the midst of the festive madness.

Pause

God,
who speaks to us
in angels' words
and a baby's cries,
speak to us this night
as we await your good word for our souls.

Pause

And as forgiven people,
we will be still
and wait,
and we will praise you.
Amen

Alison Adam

STIRRING UP MEMORIES

I made my first Christmas cake over forty years ago, in the days when I lived in a student bedsit. Thereafter, it became a sort of annual ritual. My Baby Belling was too small to bake a Christmas cake in, so I had to 'borrow' the oven of friends who shared a flat and enjoyed the luxury of a full-size cooker. The timing was crucial: it had to be an evening when none of us had a prior engagement! It became a social event in its own right, as my friends helped to chop cherries and grate lemon peel and we all cleaned out the bowl. Then came the icing – and I still have black and white photos to show the effort that went into that.

Of course I couldn't take my cake home. Grandmother would have been mortally offended. In our family she, and only she, did the baking – especially at Christmas. So the cake would languish in its tin until the start of the new term. Then, providing the grant cheques had arrived, friends would descend with bottles of sweet Spanish sauterne and hunks of cheese. This was Yorkshire where it is sacrilege to eat fruitcake without cheese. I can still see us all sitting on the floor in front of the sputtering gas fire, putting the world to rights.

The years passed and the friends changed, but still I made my Christmas cake. I married, and the icing became less elaborate as other things competed for my time.

Then came the year when Stephen, my son, made his first cake, while I sat, heavily pregnant, and supervised. The decoration was rather rudimentary, but the pleasure and the sense of achievement were immense. He still eats Christmas cake in wedges rather than slices.

As Julian and, later, Jenny came along, the making and icing of 'the cake' became a family ritual. Gradually the children moved through stirring and making a wish, to moulding marzipan holly leaves, and finally to taking full responsibility for it.

Now my children have all left home; and so, once again, it is I who make the cake. It's still the same recipe that has served me so well for over forty years. But instead of my children, it is a much-loved grandson who I hope will come to 'lay down the snow' for Santa's rather battered sledge.

Marjorie L Tolchard

CHOPPED FRUIT AND STICKY FINGERS

God of the years,
come and meet us
through the rituals
of our preparations
for the feast of Jesus' birth.

Help us to pass on,
through chopped fruit and sticky fingers,
the story of your love and sweetness
in the living of our lives. Amen

Ruth Burgess

WITH OUR ZIMMER FRAMES*

'Hark the glad sound!' we sing,
though the organist fumbles the chords
and tremulous voices cut out
on the high notes,
leaving only the bold or foolish to venture thither.

'Awake, my soul, and with the sun' –
whose rays are invisible
on this chilly third Sunday in Advent –
shine out.
(Although the Advent candle will not light
and has to be encouraged to stand upright,
like most of the twelve assorted souls,
duly awake but enclosed in their box-pews
in this ancient country church
among wind-blown fields.)

'Redeem thy misspent youth that's past.'
Plaster flakes above the pulpit;
disgrace threatens as we try to sing,
but re-infect each other with helpless, shoulder-shaking giggles
at the improbable image (gasp again!)
of our corporate misspent youth
(at 60, we are the youngest).

Isaiah proclaims much joy for the redeemed,
a holy highway, too,
which,
with our zimmer frames,
we will pursue
resolutely.

Come, Lord Jesus.

Rosie Watson

* *Gaudete Sunday in the Church of King Charles the Martyr, Shelland, Suffolk*

JOURNEYING TOWARDS CHRISTMAS IN A FRAGILE WORLD
(from a reflection)

The Lord's servant will bring lasting justice to all. He will not lose hope or courage; he will establish justice on the earth. Distant lands eagerly wait for his teaching.
Isaiah 42:3–4

Someone must answer for all these deaths.
A mother of a Black Watch soldier killed in Iraq

Born in poverty
Died in custody
In an age of technology
Graffiti on an office tower in downtown Brisbane, Australia

On the November morning of George Bush's re-election I thought of these words, written by an Aboriginal person on a wall of a glittering office block in downtown Brisbane. These powerful words say so much about our interconnected, yet strangely disconnected, world. It seems like a cliché, but we certainly live in fragile times, permeated with a range of new uncertainties for our planet and ourselves. Many of the familiar markers are moving. For millions of our sisters and brothers, these are dark days. And into this reality breaks the message of the first Christmas morning – God's surprising response to a world in need.

And for those of us who believe in an engaged Christianity, which takes seriously the strange pluralities and ambiguities of these times, the question remains: How do we celebrate the amazingly good news of the incarnation while remaining in touch with this suffering which touches into the daily lives of perhaps the majority of our sisters and brothers? That is a huge question. It's clear that we cannot celebrate Christmas in some kind of false comfort, rich in Tesco goodies, disconnected from the world's suffering. And we certainly cannot retreat into a superficial Christian fundamentalism, which regards the world as essentially a 'dark place' that must be left behind at all costs ...

When I worked in the East end of Glasgow, we had a poster in the church which said simply: Let Go, Let God. As I rushed around, busy with many things, I sometimes thought on these words, and questioned them. Since then my journey has taken me to live in different cultures. It was in India, our home for several years, that I began to learn (albeit very slowly) what it really means to 'let go', while, at the same time, being engaged with the situation around me. (Given the realities of everyday life in India, if you didn't learn to 'let go' – dozens of times a day – you would go insane!)

The late Bede Griffiths, a Benedictine monk who was both a mentor and a special friend, often spoke about discovering 'the other half of his soul' through living in South India. It was not that the intellectual, academic Bede rejected his rational, analytical side, but, rather, that the culture and temper of India allowed his more intuitive nature to also inform his actions and judgement, allowing that flow of the soul to propel him to a deeper awareness of the actual realities that surrounded his life in rural Tamil Nadu. Father Bede was one of the most engaged and compassionate people I have met, yet when you were with him you always felt that his life, thoughts and actions were earthed in that mystery of God's embrace. Somewhere along the line he had 'let go and let God' – a fact which made Bede totally present to every encounter and to the world's pain.

In these days of preparation before Christmas, the Spirit invites us to let go. A letting go of our often over-active minds so that our souls can more clearly illumine our understanding of these confused times, in which both people and the Earth are screaming in pain. A moment to be still and to listen to God; a moment of engaged listening, of being centred in our depths.

Thomas Merton, who never saw any disconnection between allowing the Spirit to infuse our thinking and radical social action, wrote, *'Prayer and meditation have an important part to play in opening up new ways and new horizons. If our prayer is the expression of a deep and grace-inspired desire for newness of life, and not the mere blind attachment to what has always been familiar and safe, God will act in us and through us in ways we cannot yet imagine or understand.'[1]*

A few weeks ago, I had the privilege of being with young people in Khayelitsha, a vast informal settlement close to Cape Town's glittering centre. All of them were HIV positive, and many of them were orphans. We know the story of AIDS in Africa, and this was its local face. A smiling face, despite the pain.

From the moment I was with them, I felt my heart to be at peace. My soul was rested. All that was required of me in that situation was to be a person of love, of gentleness, accepting of my own vulnerability, my own uncertainties. We were wounded together. Yet we were all alive and open to the new day. It was our extraordinary, rich, laughter-filled humanity that we could offer one another. I knew that I was in a sacred space and that the mystery of God's intimate goodness held us all. I thought on Mary's words: 'He has filled the hungry with good things, and sent the rich away with empty hands.' (Luke 1:53)

To allow myself in that situation to be nothing else but a person of tender love is not for a moment to forget that AIDS in Africa is earthed in injustice. It is not to deny the fact that these young people are the companions of a poverty we cannot even begin to imagine. It is not to escape from my own involvement in global suffering. Far from it.

Yet as I think about the incarnation, I know that if I am unable to let go in tender love, with an unpredictable, open-ended vulnerability, I am unable to discover fresh vision. In a real sense, I am unable to engage in the struggle and to question the prevailing assumptions of society.

As Christmas dawns on a divided world, we all know there are no quick fixes – not for the mum in Scotland who weeps for her soldier son; not for my Aboriginal friends in Queensland; not for Sipo, Xolani, Bulelwa, Thandeka and Zukile in that South African township of Khayelitsha. And, like them, I also know that some days are long and hard and dark. Yet again I come back to a reality which I have encountered time without number: It is the fact that it is often in these places of greatest suffering that God's Spirit is most powerfully present.

Which brings us back to Mary's song: a song of profound hope for the whole world. A song that arose from a contemplative heart – a surrendered heart, a soul which was somehow in tune with God's purposes. A heart rich in tender compassion. It was the song of a person who was prepared to 'let go and let God'. But it was also a song for the revolution, for liberation, for radical change and for the coming of God's upside down Kingdom. It announced great good news, but news which would not be comforting for some. Unless they changed.

And so is it possible, in these frenetic times, once again to embark on the journey of surrender – the surrendering of our souls to the One who created us and makes us whole, the Healer of nations; to sit quietly with the great biblical passages which connect Advent and Christmas, perhaps to read Mary's song of praise slowly each day, followed by some time of deep quiet; to move more deeply into the mystery of Christ's presence with us, not as an exercise in piety but as a way of restoring laughter, tender love and risk-taking into our engaged Christianity; to examine again our own prejudices, fears and shattered hopes; to hold these uncertain times in our hearts, but not feel powerless; to weep, but also to leap with joy; to hear again the voice of Isaiah and other prophets, and to walk with their words?

When I was in Jerusalem in May I asked Mordechai Vanunu what had kept him going through his long years of solitary confinement in an Israeli jail. He quietly replied that Christ had given him strength each day. I understood. For I also believe, along with many others, in a God who is present on Earth and who is active within human history.

And that God, tenderly, entered our human condition in a particular way at the back of a Bethlehem inn two thousand years ago. Knowing that, we can welcome Christmas morning with both laughter and tears, as a people of love – prepared to let go and let God transform us again.

Prayer

May my soul be rested, Lord, this Christmas –
not in flight from your amazing world,
but because I would still like to have energy
to struggle for justice,
to tell others about you,
to share what I have,
to laugh and to love,
and not be totally burnt out!

Peter Millar

[1] Thomas Merton: *Contemplation in a World of Action*, Doubleday, New York, 1973.

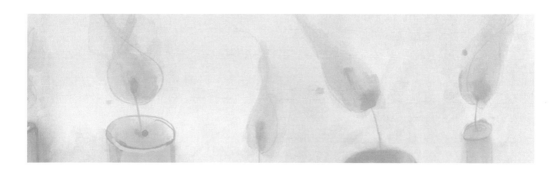

COME, GOD-WITH-US

Come, God-with-us:
who braves our rejection and hurt,
who holds us in acceptance and love.

Come, God-for-us:
who whispers
in our ears
that we –
each of us –
are beloved children.

Come, God-under-us:
who cradles us in arms that never grow weary;
whose lap has room enough
for all.

Come, God-over-us:
who watches
in the long silence of the night,
that we might rest in peace.

Come, God-beside-us:
who steadies us
when we falter,
who lifts us up
when we fall.

Come, God-behind-us:
who picks up all the faded dreams
we drop along the way
and patchworks them into hope.

O Come, O Come, Immanuel:
and we will rejoice for ever!

Thom M Shuman

PROPHETS

A PRAYER FOR THE PROPHETS

Lord God,
we bless you for those who,
without much light but with great longing,
looked for the coming of salvation for the whole human race,
and, through suffering and joy,
through harsh oppression and hard-won freedom,
at great cost and with great resilience,
prepared for the Day.
For we have entered into their joy
and by their stripes we are being healed.
Thanks be to God. Amen

Ian M Fraser

YOU BROOD OF VIPERS!

From a sermon

(Philippians 4:4–7; Luke 3:7–18)

John the Baptist – strong stuff. He's not really into pastoral counselling, is he? He must have missed that course at theological college, old John the Baptist. People come to see him and ask him what they should do. They are aware that something is wrong – and he tells them. No flattery, no feel-good ministry here! 'You brood of vipers!'

But people respect him; they seek him out. He's been through it, emptied himself of privilege – temple boy dropout – left the safety of institutional religion and found God in the wilderness. 'What should we do?' they ask. They are seeking authentic leadership, and he gives it to them.

John the Baptist is all about judgement and truth. Now, judgement isn't popular (particularly among liberal Christians), and truth is pretty hard to swallow. The idea of judgement, well, we're not really into that. 'Jesus is different from John the Baptist.' Yes, but we can't rush to Jesus's way without going through John the Baptist's. That's the whole point of why John the Baptist is there. John the Baptist is clearly in the tradition of the Old Testament prophets, the prophets who were there to tell the people where they were going wrong. We've got to listen to John the Baptist – over and over and over again. We need to know that the world is in a state of sin. We need to know that we need to repent. We need to understand that things need to be different.

What is John's challenge to the people who come to see him? What does he actually say? To those who have accumulated wealth: 'If you have two coats, give one away.' To the tax collectors, those who are living and working in the corrupt system: 'Stop being corrupt.' To soldiers: 'Stop bullying.' Now that's for the people who gathered around John the Baptist in the first century, but how might he speak to us today?

To those who come to John today, knowing their lives are empty, despite their credit cards and all their shopping therapy, John says: 'Stop trying to bolster up your own worth by accumulating material goods – give things away.'

What about the tax collectors of our time? The loan sharks, the rip-off shops offering easy credit, preying on the poor. Or the World Trade bureaucrats? (We are told that two-thirds of third world debt has been written off but, in fact, only 10% has been written off; and even then, in terms of what governments actually have to pay back, this makes very little difference to the lives of poor people. For every £1 we, in the 'first world', give in aid, we take back £2 through unfair trade.)

To the loan sharks and World Trade bureaucrats, who recognise the inequality of the system but feel powerless to know what to do, John the Baptist says: 'The system is corrupt – get out!'

And what does John say about our crazy so-called war on terror, and the increasing militarisation of our world? What does John say to the young men and women who are caught up in wars, joining the military through lack of alternatives? Those who become the soldiers of empire; those soldiers who were ordered to torture and abuse prisoners in Abu Grahib and Guantanamo Bay – surely it is to them that John speaks – those who arrive home with troubled hearts and dreadful memories of what they have done. John says: 'Do not torture, do not abuse. You are worth more than that.'

We need to hear John's judgement on our accumulation, on our corruption and on our militarism. John's message is 'Get yourself straight, get the world straight, because the end of the world is coming, and God's judgement is coming. And this geezer, Jesus, is coming and, by God, will he sort you out!'

John asks us to step into the river Jordan and be washed clean of our complicity and involvement with empire and exploitation. And then he points to Jesus. 'Behold, the lamb of God.'

John prepares the way and then Jesus steps in. And what are we given in Jesus? We are given something that's beyond prophetic, that's beyond simple honest judgement and truth-telling. We are given someone who points to models of the Kingdom, not to an end world; who says to all those who feel things are wrong: 'Look at the poor widow who puts her coin in the box. Look at her. She is the Kingdom. Look at this man, a leper, who has such faith despite what he has faced. He is the Kingdom. Look at this child. This child is an image of the Kingdom of God. Look at this woman, outcast because she is 'unclean', she has such faith; she is the Kingdom of God.' Jesus says, 'Look at these people and see and learn and know what God is about. Look at me. Look at me on the cross and understand that we are not talking about a God of power. We are talking about a God of vulnerability and love. Meet me in the resurrection. Meet me despite your violence. I offer you a new relationship – more than just an opportunity to start again. Do not fear condemnation. Hear the judgement, hear truth, hear wisdom – and know my reconciliation, which is the way of love. Be filled with my grace. Stop. Choose. And step into my love and be empowered by grace. I am here to show you a God who turns the world upside down. A world that you can turn upside down too.'

No condemnation there. Judgement certainly. But judgement matched with grace. When you hear Jesus's judgement, you don't shy away in guilt and fear. You are filled with grace, in order to live the truth, to be witnesses to his love.

And that's the coming of the Kingdom: living out the love and justice of God as shown in Jesus. The Kingdom, as John said, is nigh. The end of the world as we know it is only an action away. When we act, filled with God's grace, for love and justice, when we step into changing our world, the end of the world, the Kingdom, has come – in our hearts, in our actions.

The end of the world as we know it comes in our acts of compassion and justice and love. It comes when, open to Christ, we are full of the Spirit of the upside down Kingdom in our hearts and live it out in our lives …

Ray Gaston

THE VOICE OF GOD

The voice of God is the voice crying out for justice:
    the voice aching for wholeness;
    the voice ranging ahead of us,
    inviting us to stand fast for justice,
    caressing our vulnerability,
    tempting us to become whole.

In stillness, let us seek to become open to the voice of God.

We pray:
With people who only hear tormenting voices
raging inside their heads … self-destructive voices,
oppressive voices saying, 'You're no good',
'You're wicked', 'You're no one' …

For people whose voices boom so loudly
they imagine they speak with the voice of God;
for multinational corporations,
dictators and bullies, politicians lost in their own self-importance,
countries who imagine they have a special calling from God …

With those whose voices don't seem to count;
whose mouths move, but no one listens.
Whose voices can't penetrate the plate glass of our indifference …

For ourselves: who are assaulted by a Babel of voices telling us,
'You need this', 'You want that',
'Buy this product, you'll be more popular.
You'll be more beautiful.'

In silence, we strain to hear the voice of God.

Silence (extended)

Out of the troubles of silence gather us,
Voice of God:
agitate and excite us,
startle us with your unexpected presence,
ready us to act for justice. Amen

Rachel Mann

REMEMBERING

The women in the genealogy of Jesus

We remember the daughters of Tamar:
women pushed away and denied their rights,
who use their bodies and their sexuality,
who deceive and manipulate
to survive and give birth to the future.
WE REMEMBER THEIR PAIN AND STRUGGLE.
WE CELEBRATE THEIR PART IN GOD'S STORY.

We remember the daughters of Rahab:
women despised and held in contempt,
who put aside established loyalties

to give harbour and refuge to the stranger,
struggling to ensure a future for their families.
WE REMEMBER THEIR PAIN AND STRUGGLE.
WE CELEBRATE THEIR PART IN GOD'S STORY.

We remember the daughters of Bathsheba:
women taken by force for lust or profit,
separated and torn from those they love,
facing loss and heartache,
rebuilding life in the midst of grief.
WE REMEMBER THEIR PAIN AND STRUGGLE.
WE CELEBRATE THEIR PART IN GOD'S STORY.

We remember the daughters of Mary:
women facing scandal and disrespect,
saying 'yes' to an unknown future
and the mystery of God's promise,
bearing in their bodies the saving of the world.
WE REMEMBER THEIR PAIN AND STRUGGLE.
WE CELEBRATE THEIR PART IN GOD'S STORY.

Jan Berry

ANNA'S STORY

Narrator: In the Temple in Jerusalem there was a prophetess. She was well on in years, having lived with her husband for seven years after her marriage before becoming a widow. She was now in her eighties and never left the Temple, serving God day and night with fasting and prayer. *(Luke 2:36 –37)*

Anna: Me, I'm Anna. I'm old now, spending my time in the Temple praying, putting my life into the hands of my maker day by day.

I wasn't always old; I was young once, and beautiful. I married young, and what a wedding! My parents were important people. There were no expenses spared. The best wine, the choicest food, the most revered rabbi; a day to remember, to cherish, to bring a moment of warmth into my old bones.

He died young, my bridegroom, before we'd been blessed with children. Surrounded by my married friends, I was dressed in widow's mourning. Different, pitied, a person not to be included in the guest list, unless a suitable chaperone could be found.

I came to the Temple seeking strength and consolation, and I found it, through the lonely nights and daytime hours, through the moments and months and years.

And here I am, eighty-four years old and in the Temple praying, lots of stories and memories, a lifetime of believing, an aging mind and body, a bit forgetful sometimes, but few regrets.

Over there, that's Simeon. I see him often. He's a good man people tell me, kind and generous, a keeper of the commandments, a good friend to the poor. He told me once that God had told him that before he died he would see the Messiah. So he's waiting for God to keep his promise. He comes to the Temple each day to pray and to listen, and to wait for the Messiah to come. He's a good man, Simeon, and faithful. I hope God answers his prayers soon.

It's getting busy in the city with so many people coming here for the census. It seems like the whole world must have been born in Jerusalem, and they're all coming home. It's all right for the strong ones, the young ones. They can cope with all the hustle and bustle. But what about the weak and the sick? What about the small children, the women who are pregnant? What about the ones like me, the old ones? I wouldn't like to be travelling now.

I'd better stop talking to you and start talking to God. Praying is something I can still do and it makes me feel useful. There's a lot of people today who'll be needing my prayers.

Ruth Burgess

COME, GOD

Come, God.
Come with the frightened.
Come with the poor.
Come with the children.
Come with those who have always been your friends.
Come and lead us to where you are living,
and show us what you want us to do.

Ruth Burgess

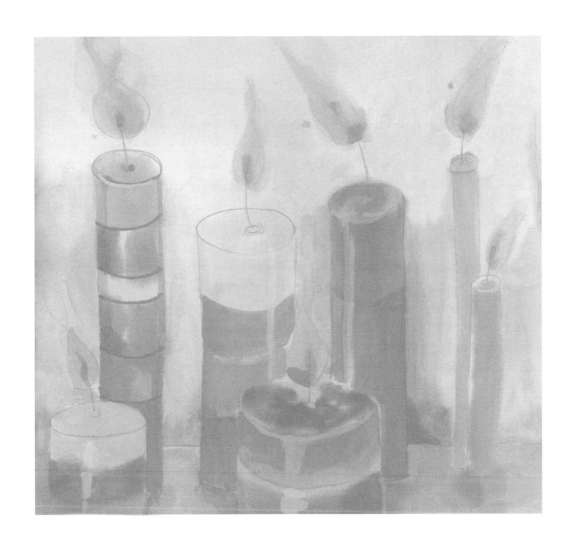

ENTER THE ANGELS

MAGNIFICAT MOMENTS

From a sermon

I like to think of Magnificat moments, when you actually do see the powerful brought down, and the lowly raised up. There are moments when that happens. I'm sure there are stories that we can all tell. I had an experience this week – a Magnificat moment. I was in court with someone who was charged with assaulting two police officers. And the truth of the story is that it was the other way round. There were four police officers giving evidence and this one person, on their own, with a line of magistrates. And slowly, as the trial proceeded, the prosecution's case unravelled. It fell apart. The police were quite clearly lying. And they tripped over themselves. The lies were revealed. And it was beautiful to watch. I had to stay in the court to wait for this person to give their evidence, because, I thought, if four of them sit there then it's going to be quite intimidating. And quite the opposite happened. The person was able to speak out, speak the truth, speak very movingly and, in comparison with how the police had given their evidence, it was just so obvious that this was truth-telling. And what you actually saw was that this person was raised up. In the court, you could actually see the magistrates completely and utterly believing it. The whole thing was revealed. A powerful Magnificat moment. And there was shame on the police officers' faces. As this evidence was being given, it was quite clearly seen that they were being exposed. The lowly were raised up. The person who was despised, who was actually being abused that day, was raised up. And those who were powerful were brought low. They turned up in their uniforms, but they were shamed. I was sitting there in the court, wanting to shout out 'Praise the Lord!' I wanted to sing the Magnificat, because it really was that kind of moment.

Ray Gaston

ON THE ROAD

Mary: Oh Elizabeth, have you heard the news?
Elizabeth: What, about you being pregnant? Of course I have – you told me weeks ago!
Mary: No, not that. About the census?
Elizabeth: Oh yes, *The Herald* has been full of that for weeks.

Mary: Yes, but it means Joseph and I have to go to Bethlehem.

Elizabeth: Why Bethlehem, of all places?

Mary: Well, that's where Joseph's family comes from.

Elizabeth: Oh yes, of course – I'd forgotten he was a southerner. But how on earth are you going to manage it – it will be about the time the baby's due, won't it?

Mary: Yes, and I'm dreading it.

Elizabeth: Do you have to go? Surely there are exemptions for pregnant women, or old people, or people who are ill?

Mary: No, I've checked – we have to register in person. And you know what it's like these days if you don't have the correct papers or I.D. – it's as if you don't exist.

Elizabeth: What stupid red tape. How are you going to get there? The Virgin trains won't be running, surely?

Mary: No, not at this time of year – probably sand on the line or something! So I think it will have to be the Donkey Express – and you know how long that takes.

Elizabeth: Oh, what an awful journey. And with the baby due at any time. And goodness knows what dangers on the way – robbers, and drunken soldiers abusing you at checkpoints and –

Mary: (interrupting) Oh, don't! You're really cheering me up! I just hope we can get there before the baby arrives. We should be all right; but if he comes early I don't know what we'll do. And I don't know what accommodation we'll find. Bethlehem's such a small town, I'm sure it will be packed out.

Elizabeth: You'll probably end up sharing a stable with a donkey!

Mary: Thanks very much! I suppose I'm just hoping that, if this baby is really so special, God will take care of us.

Elizabeth: I'm not sure I'd rely on that. You would think he could arrange things better in the first place. If he's God, why couldn't he do something about the timing of the census?

Mary: I don't know. There's so much I don't understand about this business. It just seems to me that God wants this baby to experience the same mess and muddle as everyone else in this mixed-up world – even if that means being born on the road. And somehow I don't think the journey will get any easier as he grows up.

Jan Berry

ELIZABETH – A MONOLOGUE

Pregnant!
At my age!
I thought it was the menopause.
Wow, did I get that wrong!

Pregnant.

Why me?
What have I done to deserve this?

Zech, my husband, he's no help at the moment.

They brought him home from the Temple a few weeks ago, said he'd had a funny turn, a stroke maybe, and he couldn't tell them what had happened.

I put him to bed with an extra blanket and some warmed wine, and he seemed all right the next morning, but still not able to speak. Very odd.

The neighbours keep knocking and asking how he's doing:
Such a shame that Zech isn't able to preach at the moment.
He's such a good speaker.
The synagogue doesn't seem the same without him.

Still, at least it keeps them off asking how I am. They'd never believe me if I told them!

I finally got up enough courage to tell Zech that I'm pregnant. I thought that the shock might get him talking again, but it didn't.

He smiled when I told him, a knowing kind of smile, and then he got all excited and tried to tell me something. He kept standing up and flapping his arms up and down, and then putting his hand on my stomach and nodding. Heaven knows what all that was about!

When I think about it, there have been other women like me, pregnant years after they should have been; Sarah and Mrs Manoah, I wonder how they coped.

They both had boys; I wonder what mine will be. I'd rather have a girl, but maybe God only sends boys to older women, though I can't think why. A daughter to support us in our old age would be far more useful. A daughter to share things with would be wonderful, especially if Zech doesn't recover his speech.

I suppose I'd better think about maternity clothes and buying some things for the baby. Although I don't really want to go shopping yet. All the neighbours would start asking questions. And I can't send Zech in his present state – imagine him trying to mime baby oil and nappies to the shop assistant!

Mary, my cousin, is coming to stay next week, a nice lass, her husband is a joiner. And I know he's making her a cradle in preparation for when they get married and start a family.

Perhaps I could persuade her to lend it to me. I don't suppose they'll be needing it for a while yet.

Maybe when they're married she'll have a girl too. They could be company for each other. Think of it, two wee girls growing up together, descendants of Tamar and Ruth, true daughters of Israel. The world would be truly blessed.

Ruth Burgess

WE LIFT OUR HEARTS IN PRAISE

Lord, we lift our hearts in praise to you, ~~seeking to learn from the example of Mary,~~ *as we seek to learn from the examples of the prophets and Mary & Joseph.*
glad that you are our Saviour
and that you remember us, your lowly servants.

We praise you for calling humans to do your work in the world,
for choosing ordinary people to do extraordinary deeds.

We praise you for your holy name,
known to generations,
and we praise you for the mercy you show
to those who honour you.

We praise you for the workings of justice,
when the mighty and proud have been brought down,
when the lowly and hungry have been lifted and fed,
and the rich made to realise the emptiness of material things.

We praise you for the promises you have kept
and place our trust in you for the continuing promises which you make

to all the descendants of Abraham,
to all who follow you and seek to obey your commands.

We hold before you the shame we feel for our faults,
knowing that so often we fail to respond to your calling.
Often our excuses seem to be good ones,
but when we think of someone like Mary –
willing to risk her life and reputation –
we become more aware of the conditions
we attach to our willingness to serve.
You call us each in different ways,
according to our abilities and potential.
Forgive us when we identify with
the mighty and proud rather than the lowly and hungry.
Forgive us and call us once again to do your will.

As we move closer to the celebration of your birth,
help us to accept you as Mary did –
wholeheartedly,
willing to expect and accept the unexpected,
prepared to trust your way rather than the ways of the world –
that we may continue as children of Abraham and followers of Christ, for ever.

Amen

Liz Gibson

MAGNIFICAT FOR TWO VOICES*

My soul proclaims the greatness of the Lord,
My spirit rejoices in God my Saviour.

I'm pregnant.

For you, Lord, have looked with favour on your lowly servant.

I'm 14 and I'm pregnant.

You, the Almighty, have done great things for me
And holy is your name.

Mum'll kill me.

You have mercy on those who fear you,
From generation to generation.

I'll get rid of it. Before it shows. She'll never know.

You have shown strength with your arm
And scattered the proud in their conceit.

I'll know.

Casting down the mighty from their thrones
And lifting up the lowly.

Help me. Please, help me.

You have filled the hungry with good things
And sent the rich away empty.

It's not fair.

You have come to the aid of your servant Israel
To remember the promise of mercy.

It's just not fair.

The promise made to our forebears,
To Abraham and his children for ever

I'm 14 and I'm pregnant.

Rachel Mann

*This piece has been used in a youth-centred context and can be used as a springboard for open-ended discussion. It works especially well as a dramatic piece, where the words of the Magnificat are simply read and the other words are 'performed' by a young adult. This requires decent acting skills but is worth the attempt.

GESTATION OF GOD

Awesome
Angel news
God in me

Flesh of my flesh

Gabriel
Inviting my assent

I say yes.

Beryl Jeanne

GOOD ENOUGH
(Matthew 1:18–23)

Joseph: I've had enough!
           This would try the patience of a saint;
           and I don't think I'm a saint,
           just a man of principle.
           Just an ordinary mortal
           minding my own business –
           Joiner and General Household Repairs –
           trying to do my best
           with the gifts God gives me:
           Behold the handyman of the Lord!

           Folk appreciate good workmanship.
           On the whole they respect me:
           a solid member of the community.
           I never set out to be clever
           but want to do what's right.
           And now this –
           what will people say?

           Mary – my intended –
           she's going to have a baby.
           It's not mine.
           It can't be mine.
           What will people say?
           Nazareth is a small town:

Everyone knows everyone else's business.
This isn't going to be good for trade:
I'll be a laughing stock.
I'll call the wedding off,
quietly of course,
that must be the right thing.

Angel:	Joseph!
Joseph:	That's me. Joinery and General Household Repairs, prompt service and cash terms. Who called?
Angel:	I did.
Joseph:	Who are you?
Angel:	An angel of the Lord.
Joseph:	I must be dreaming.
Angel:	You are.
Joseph:	I must be getting back to work.
Angel:	Joseph, will you just listen? – you're as thick as two short planks.
Joseph:	It's likely in my line of work. Well, what do you want?
Angel:	You are a descendant of David?
Joseph:	Yes, you see, David begat Solomon and Solomon, Rehoboam, who begat Abijah, who begat Asa, who begat Jehoshaphat …
Angel:	Thank you. Do not be afraid to take Mary to be your wife.
Joseph:	But …
Angel:	For it is by the Holy Spirit that she has conceived.
Joseph:	Well, I never …
Angel:	I know. It was an immaculate conception. She will give birth to a son and you shall name him –
Joseph:	Jehoshaphat?
Angel:	No – Jesus.
Joseph:	What kind of name is that?
Angel:	Jesus – for he will save his people from their sins.
Joseph:	What, all our family? All the people in Nazareth? All God's people? All the people in New Mills?* One little baby?

Angel: Yes, and so it will come true
what the Lord said through the prophet:
A virgin will become pregnant
and give birth to a son
and he will be called Emmanuel.

Joseph: But you told me to call him 'Jesus'.
I can't understand all this.
I'm good with my hands, not with words –
just a manual worker.

Angel: Emmanuel is a special name.
It means 'God is with us'.

Joseph: What, with the workers?
With the people of Nazareth?
With the people of New Mills?*
With ordinary folk like me?
'God with us' – that's good enough for me.
Mary! Mary! …
We're going to have a baby!

Jan Sutch Pickard

Substitute the name of your own community.

ANGEL VOICES

Opening responses

Reader: Just when life seems cosy
and comfortably predictable:

ALL: ANGELS APPEAR UNEXPECTEDLY,
AND POINT US IN DIRECTIONS
WE WOULD NOT HAVE CHOSEN.

Reader: Just when we have reached the point
of comforting assurance in our respectability:

ALL: ANGELS APPEAR UNEXPECTEDLY,
AND POSE UNCOMFORTABLE QUESTIONS
WE WOULD NOT HAVE CHOSEN TO FACE.

Reader: And when we have followed the pointings of angels
       and answered their disquieting questions
       and we feel that things can't get any worse:
ALL: ANGELS APPEAR UNEXPECTEDLY,
       AND REMIND US THAT 'ALL SHALL BE WELL,
       AND ALL SHALL BE WELL,
       AND ALL MANNER OF THING SHALL BE WELL'.*

Reader: For the God of love works to good in all who fear Him.
ALL: THE GOD OF LOVE WORKS TO GOOD
       IN ALL WHO DARE TO LISTEN FOR ANGELS.

Scripture reading(s) – Luke 1:8–20 (Zechariah); Luke 1:26–38 (Mary); Matthew 1:18–24 (Joseph); Luke 2:8–20 (shepherds)

Carols

Closing responses

Reader: You speak to your people through angels.
ALL: KEEP OUR EARS AND HEARTS OPEN
       TO THE WHISPERS OF ANGEL VOICES

Reader: Angels come among us
       and many have entertained them unawares.
ALL: KEEP US WATCHFUL AND WAITING
       FOR THE SPIRIT BEINGS IN OUR MIDST;
       TEACH US TO RECOGNISE THEM
       IN ALL THEIR DISGUISES.

Reader: Angels come among us,
       their presence comforting or disquieting.
ALL: MAKE US SENSITIVE TO THEIR PRESENCE,
       FEELING THEM GUIDING US INTO THE FUTURE;
       LEADING US TO HEAVEN,
       WHERE WE WILL SEE AND HEAR CLEARLY
       WHAT WE HAVE GLIMPSED IN SHADOW.

From Wellspring

*Julian of Norwich

JOSEPH

Hullo! Can I speak to God please?
Joseph Davidson, Carpenter of Nazareth here.
Are you there, Lord?
'Speak Lord, for thy servant heareth.'

Oh my God! I've a problem.
I need help – and quickly.
'Bow down thy ear to hear me, O Lord.
Save thy servant who trusteth in thee.'

Remember that job you asked me to do for you?
It was pretty dodgy, taking on Mary like that.
I did it as a favour to you,
and I thought I deserved just a wee bit consideration.

Maybe I should not have done,
but I'm only human … but anyway.
Now everything has gone wrong.
I dread to think what will go wrong next.

They gey nearly stoned wee Mary;
if you don't mind me saying so – it was hellish.
I'd never realised how cruel and nasty
religious people could be. It fair puts you off.

Now I'm the laughing stock of the place.
Are you there? Where were you?
I've seen more angels in the past few weeks
than most folk do in a lifetime, and I'm grateful, mind!

But I could do with some practical, down-to-earth help.
'It is time for thee to work, O Lord.'
Then there was our house … building's my job,
I ken about building houses. I've built dozens.

But my apprentice got 'flu, the weather turned nasty,
and my supplier let me down.
'Except the Lord build the house
they labour in vain that build it.'
Well, I dinna ken where you were in that building!

And once I had got it built … what happened?
I'm ready to get Mary installed in time for the baby coming
and those bloody Romans need to count us.
So … it's on your donkey, boy … back to Bethlehem.

My poor old donkey's not up to that sort of thing;
and as for poor Mary, could you have no consideration for her?
All the bed and breakfasts on the road were booked,
and my donkey broke down, of course.

'Awake O Lord, why sleepest thou?'
(That old psalmist knew a thing or two!)
'O that thou wouldst rend the heavens and come down!'
But there's no sign of you anywhere.

It was good to see the old place again;
but seeing Mary's condition, nobody wanted to know.
So here is your faithful servant,
In this stinking, rotten stable, literally in the shit.

Ian Cowie

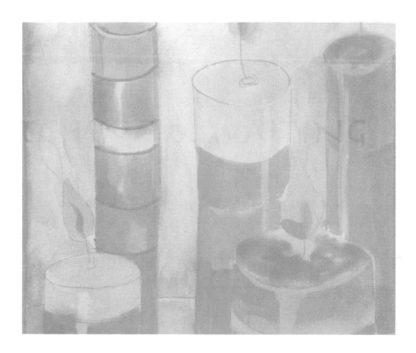

CHOOSING GOD

Choosing God.

Choosing to let your child be born in poverty
and of doubtful parentage.

Choosing an occupied country with unstable rulers.

Choosing the risk of him dying in a dirty stable
after a long journey by a pregnant teenager.

Choosing to let him grow up poor, and in danger,
and misunderstood by those who loved him.

Choosing God,
we doubt the wisdom of your choices then,
and we doubt them now,
while the rich are still full
and it is the poor who get sent empty away.

Help us, lest we, in our anger or ignorance,
choose to walk another way.

Ruth Burgess

CHRISTINGLE SERVICE

CHRISTINGLE SERVICE

The ideal seating arrangement for this service would be to set out four sides of chairs – East, West, North, South – and a central table with the component parts of the Christingle on it.

During the service each member of the congregation will be invited to make a Christingle. To make the Christingles you will need: oranges, red bands (pre-cut lengths of red insulating tape), 'fruits' (cocktail sticks with sweeties on them – it's easier not to include nuts, as is sometimes done, because of nut allergies, and because they are difficult to spear on a stick!). Over-estimate the number of Christingles you will need.

You will also need a supply of candles, one for each member of the congregation.

The date you hold the Christingle service will determine the number of Advent candles you will need to light.

This service lends itself especially to a multimedia approach, with two or more projectors, enabling the congregation to dispense entirely with holding printed papers.

Introduction: The worship leader gives an introduction to the service, including what a Christingle is and the history of Christingle.

Call to worship

(Readings come from the four sides of the congregation as indicated – East, West, North, South.)

Reader (EAST):   In the beginning everything was engulfed in total darkness of the deep ... God commanded: 'Let there be light.' *(Genesis 1:1–3)*

The first Advent candle is lit.

Chant: On God alone I wait silently (John L. Bell, *Psalms of Patience, Protest and Praise*, Wild Goose Publications, or *There is One Among Us*, Wild Goose Publications)

Reader (WEST):   The people who walked in darkness have seen a great light. *(Isaiah 9:2)*

The second Advent candle is lit.

Chant: On God alone I wait silently

Reader (NORTH): The light shines in the darkness, and the darkness will never put it out. *(John1:5)*

The third Advent Candle is lit.

Chant: On God alone I wait silently

Reader (SOUTH): Let us walk in the light God gives us. *(Isaiah 2:5)*

Chant: On God alone I wait silently

The fourth Advent Candle is lit.

EAST:	We come from the East.
WEST:	We come from the West.
NORTH:	We come from the North.
SOUTH:	We come from the South.
ALL:	FOR GOD INVITES US ALL AND NO ONE IS SHUT OUT. THOUGH SOME WHO ARE NOW LAST WILL BE FIRST, AND SOME WHO ARE NOW FIRST WILL BE LAST.

Prayers

Living God,
we who come from
East and West and North and South
bring to you
our heavy loads.

(Pause)

Jesus, we treat you as well
or as badly
as we treat our friends
and neighbours.
We are sorry
and we have no excuse.

(Pause)

God of mercy,
hear us, forgive us,
heal us, free us.
Give us space and silence
to hear your Word to set us free.

(Silence)

Listen, God is good.
And when we are ready to change,
from guilt to grace,
from darkness to light,
God pronounces pardon,
and grants blessing.
Thanks be to God.

ALL: AMEN

The orange

Leader: *(holding up an orange)* The orange represents the world. The world held lovingly in God's hands, from the beginning of time, and every day and night until God's work is done.

Bible reading: Psalm 95:1–5

Song: God's got the whole world in his/her hands

Action: Oranges are distributed during the song

Prayers

NORTH :   *(together)* Loving God, we thank you
for making the whole world
of which we are just a little part.

SOUTH: *(together)* Help us to love the world:
hills and valleys,
streams and seas,
birds and animals,
pets and creepy-crawlies.

WEST: *(together)* Help us to love the world,
people we like,
people we don't.

EAST: *(together)* Help us to love the world
as you love the world,
because you made us
to be like you.

ALL: AMEN

The red band

Leader: *(holding up an orange with a red band around it)* The red band around the orange represents the blood of Jesus Christ who was crucified. In the life, death and resurrection of Jesus we see God loving the world and changing people's lives for good.

Song: My song is love unknown

Action: Red bands are distributed during the song.

The fruits

Leader: Through bread and wine made from the fruits of the earth,
Jesus showed us how he would save us.
Through food and drink,
God has always shown people how he loves them.

Bible readings: Psalm 104:13,15; Mark 14:22–25

Song

Action: Fruits (sweeties) are distributed during the song.

The candle

Leader: *(holding up a lit candle)* The candle represents Christ,
who is the light of the world.
Jesus is the light that shines in the darkness.
The light that cannot be put out.

EAST:	People will come from the East.
WEST:	People will come from the West.
NORTH:	People will come from the North.
SOUTH:	People will come from the South.

ALL:	AND TAKE THEIR PLACES
	IN THE KINGDOM OF GOD:
	AND SOME
	WHO ARE NOW LAST
	WILL BE FIRST.
	AND SOME WHO ARE FIRST
	WILL BE LAST.

Song

Action: Candles are distributed during the song.

EAST:	We have come from the East.
NORTH:	We have come from the North.
WEST:	We have come from the West.
SOUTH:	We have come from the South.

ALL:	AND TOGETHER WE ASK
	THAT THE LIGHT
	THAT WE SEARCH FOR
	MAY LIGHT OUR WAY IN LOVE,
	THIS NIGHT,
	THIS CHRISTMAS,
	AND IN DAYS TO COME. AMEN

Action: Light is passed to everyone holding a Christingle, as people sing the chant *Lord of life (Common Ground)*. The singing continues until all the candles are lit.

Blessing

May the smile of God warm us,
may the light of Jesus lead us,
may the Holy Spirit blaze in our lives and fill us with love. AMEN

Closing song: Walk in the light or Christingle song (see p.219)

David Coleman

O ROUND AS THE WORLD IS THE ORANGE YOU GIVE US!

Carol for a Christingle service

(Tune: Streets of Laredo)

O round as the world is the orange you give us!
And happy are they who to Jesus belong:
So let the world know, as we join in Christingle,
That Jesus, the Hope of the World, is our song.

O bright is the flame of the candle you give us!
And happy are they who to Jesus belong:
So let the world know, as we join in Christingle,
That Jesus, the Light of the World, is our song.

Go northward or southward, go eastward or westward,
How happy are they who to Jesus belong!
So let the world know, as they join in Christingle,
That Jesus, the Peace of the World, is our song.

When homeward we go, we must take Jesus with us,
For happy are they who to Jesus belong:
So let the world know, as we join in Christingle,
That Jesus, the Saviour of all, is our song.

Fred Pratt Green

THE LONGEST NIGHT

THE LONGEST NIGHT

(This service is held on or near the longest night of the year.)

Welcome

Call to worship

Leader:	Tonight we gather here in this place of refuge,
ALL:	FOR WE ARE LOST,
	WE ARE LONELY,
	WE ARE AFRAID.

Leader:	Tonight we gather, daring to wonder
	if God has indeed come in Jesus –
	discerning the rejection we have known,
	intimate with our failed relationships,
	holding our heartache in hands of tenderness.
	Tonight we gather with neighbours and strangers,
	a family made one by our brokenness;
ALL:	COMING WITH OUR HEARTS FULL OF HOPE,
	AND OUR HEADS FILLED WITH DOUBTS.

Leader:	Tonight, we gather just as we are,
ALL:	FOR GOD HAS PROMISED TO MEET US HERE
	AND TO WELCOME US FOR WHO WE ARE.

Carol

Prayer

Holy God of Advent,
you became weak
so we would find strength in moments of heartbreak;
you left the safety of heaven
to wander the wilderness of the world,
holding our hands when we feel hopeless;
you set aside your glory
to hold our pain so we might be healed,

even when there seems to be no hope;
you became one of us,
so we would never be alone in any moment,
in any circumstance.

So come now,
Child of Bethlehem,
to strengthen us in these days.
May we feel your presence
in a way we have never known,
not just as one born in a stable
long ago and far away
but as the One born in our hearts.

You have promised to go before us:
into our brokenness, into hospital rooms,
into empty houses, into graveyards,
into our future held by God,
and you are here, even now,
waiting for each of us:
to serve us,
to hold us,
to comfort us,
to heal us,
to live in us, now and for ever. Amen

Carols: O come, O come, Emmanuel or O little town of Bethlehem (verses 1–3) or
Away in a manger

Prayers of intercession

Voice 1:   All around us are the sights and sounds of Christmas, Gentle God: the
laughter of parties, the songs of carollers, the shouts of children sledding
down hills, the music in every store. But deep within us we carry our pain;
our grief walks with us every step we take; loneliness is a shawl we drape
over our shoulders on empty nights. So, in this time when every night
stretches into eternity, we come to you, bringing our gifts: not gold,
frankincense and myrrh, but grief, bitterness and loss.

Voice 2:   We have come from different backgrounds, from different families, from
different faith traditions. But we have all lived in the land of shame and

wandered the far country of despair. We have stood on the side of every room we have gone into, hoping against hope that someone would ask us to dance but finding the wall is our only friend.

Voice 3:   In a season when so many people don't have enough hours in a day to get their lists checked off, their cards mailed, their presents wrapped, we have all the time in the world: to remember the loss that has stolen the joy of the season; to grieve over a job, a dream, a loved one; to sit in the shadows of our homes, too weary to turn on the lights; to wander the streets lit by lights on all the houses, but not by the Light of the world.

Voice 4:   Our fear of the future, our remembrance of the past, our pain that is difficult to bear and harder to release, our emptiness which cannot be filled with platitudes, our hands which cannot hold the ones we wish to embrace: all make this a season of long nights.

ALL: BE WITH US IN OUR LONELINESS, IN OUR LONGING, IN OUR LOSS, IN OUR LIVES. IN JESUS' NAME, WE PRAY. AMEN

A time of silent reflection

ASSURANCE OF OUR ACCEPTANCE BY GOD:

Carol: In the bleak midwinter (verses 1–2)

Hearing the Word of God

During the scripture readings, people are invited to come forward and light a candle. Also, a big bowl of salt water (symbolising God's tears) can be centrally placed and people can touch their fingers to the water and then touch their cheeks under their eyes, or they can 'add their tears' by taking salt from another bowl and sprinkling it into the water.

Suggested readings:
Psalm 107:4–9
Psalm 130:1–4
Matthew 8:18–20
Matthew 22:1–10

John 11:33–36
Matthew 27:45–46
Luke 2:1–7
Matthew 11:28–30
Matthew 5:1–12
Revelation 21:1–7

THE BODY OF CHRIST:

Carol: In the bleak midwinter (verses 3–4)

The great prayer of thanksgiving

Eucharist

Carol: Go, tell it on the mountain or Come, thou long-expected Jesus

Blessing

In your silence, may the Word dwell in your heart.
In your brokenness, may the Bread of Life heal you.
In your pain, may the One who can heal you touch your soul. AMEN

Carol: Silent night

People depart in silence.

Thom M Shuman

CHRISTMAS EVE

2 Sam 7:1–5, 8–12,14,16; Ps 89; Lk1: 67–79

RESPONSES FOR CHRISTMAS EVE

Opening responses

In David's town
Of David's line
JESUS OUR SAVIOUR

God clothed in flesh
Bone of our bone
JESUS OUR SAVIOUR

Promised of old
Here in our midst
JESUS OUR SAVIOUR

Closing responses

Holy and righteous
ALL OUR DAYS

Our sins forgiven
OUR DARKNESS LIGHT

Working for justice
PRAYING FOR PEACE

Holy and righteous
ALL OUR LIVES

Ruth Burgess

ADVENT HYMN

(Tune: Nativity)

Praise to the God who clears the way,
Preparing room and space;
For power and pride will lose their sway
As peace comes in their place.

Praise to the God who comes to judge
The truth of word and deed,
Calling our minds and wills to change,
Rebuking wealth and greed.

Praise to the God who waits with us
For hope and joy to reign,
Who shares our suffering and our loss,
Embodied in our pain.

Praise to the God who comes to bring
New joy to all who mourn.
The whole creation 'Glory' sings
As Christ the light is born.

Jan Berry

A POEM FOR TWO VOICES

Voice 1:   Twinkle, twinkle, little star,
how we wonder what you are.
Up above the world so high,
like a diamond in the sky.
Bringing visions from afar,
how we wonder what you are.

Voice 2:   Twinkle, twinkle, little star,
we know exactly what you are.
An incandescent ball of gas
acting like a solid mass;
by your twinkle, little star,
we can tell just what you are.

Voice 1:   Why you're shining, little star,
isn't what you really are.
Humans, made of flesh and bone,
are much more than that alone.
Go on, twinkle, little star,
just be true to what you are.

Voice 2:   Twinkle, twinkle, Christmas star,
we can work out what you are.
Star exploding deep in space
just by chance seen by our race;
you might twinkle, Christmas star,
but we know just what you are.

Voice 1:   Twinkle, twinkle, star so bright,
shining down on Christmas night.
Doesn't matter what they say,
you're the sign for Christmas Day;
Jesus came to Earth that night,
as you twinkled, star so bright.

Voice 2:   Twinkle, twinkle, star of joy,
lead us to that baby boy.
You may seem a random chance
but He placed you in the dance.
Twinkle, twinkle, star of love,
show the way to Him above.

Voice 1:   Twinkle star and shine so bright,
bathing Earth in heavenly light.
Lovers gaze and poets rhyme;
artists paint your colours fine;
in your twinkling, little star,
you remind us who we are.

Voice 2:   Some will strive to understand
stars that spread like grains of sand.

Voice 1:   Some admire their beauty bright,
lighting up our darkest night.

Voices 1 & 2:   Doesn't matter which you do,
He, who made them all, made you.

Alix Brown

IF YOU CAME IN THE SPRING

If you came in the spring,
we could expect newness,
bright yellow flowers
to soften your path,
the songs of birds
to herald your coming.

But you came in
winter's despair;
the chill of complacency
settled upon us.

If you came in summer
we could expect you
to be bronzed
blonde,
stepping from the sea.

But you came
in a stable,
a wrinkled baby
with animals as midwives,
and angels for playmates.

Help us to set down
our parcels of expectations
to reach down and scoop
you up in our arms,
your laughing breath
giving us life.
Amen

Thom M Shuman

DEAR GOD

Dear God
I hope on Christmas day my family will be happy.

I can get some new roller boots
if you will tell Father Christmas I've been good.

Love Gemma
(aged 7)

CHRISTMAS PRAYER

You came as a baby, Lord,
as a little helpless child
who relied on a human family
to care for him.

You cried because you were hungry,
because you were homeless,
because you were a stranger
far away from home.

You still cry with hunger, Lord,
in the voices of the many starving;
your tears still flow: for the homeless,
the lonely and the forgotten;
you still rely on human families
to care for you.

And so this Christmas, Lord, we pray:
help us to be the kind of people
who look for you in the world,
and joyfully discover you
as we care for one another.

Carol Dixon

CHRISTMAS EVE IN DURHAM

The grey dome of sky darkens,
and they come.
From dales and towns,
from overseas,
their tramping footsteps echoing,
merging with those who trod the same path
long ago.

Up the cobbled street
noisily they come.
Some denim-clad, bright scarves flapping,
mingling with those in dark warm coats.
Piped music bursts from warm taverns
drowning their voices,
yet still they climb
up and up
to Palace Green,
oblivious of icy air
swirling, forming ghostly shapes.

The cathedral bells ring out
inviting all to come
and, as evening stars appear,
the moving mass file quietly
through the sanctuary door.

The bells now silent as
a lone clear voice of a chorister sings out in the darkness:
'Once in royal David's city',
and all are stilled to watch
and wonder.

And so the pageant begins,
the story unfolds;
the world is changed –
a child is born.

Enid L Ayers

ANGEL DIALOGUE

Angel 1: You get all the best jobs.

Angel 2: Yours matters just as much.

Angel 1: You get to fly solo.

Angel 2: But you create strength and glory through numbers.

Angel 1: You get to talk one-to-one. That's special.

Angel 2: But your voices will fill all of the heavens.

Angel 1: You've been singled out. She's a beautiful, unique young woman. I get a group of rough men.

Angel 2: You get the whole sky to fill. I will only fill a lowly room.

Angel 1: But you will always be remembered for what you say.

Angel 2: Your song, too, will live on.

Pause

Angel 1: Maybe we've both got the best jobs.

Angel 2: This is *the* job. And we're both part of it.

Angel 1: 'Hark, the herald angels sing'

Angel 2: We're both bringing the message as heaven gives him up …

Angel 1: 'Glory to the new born King!'

Pam Hathorn and Carolyn Morris

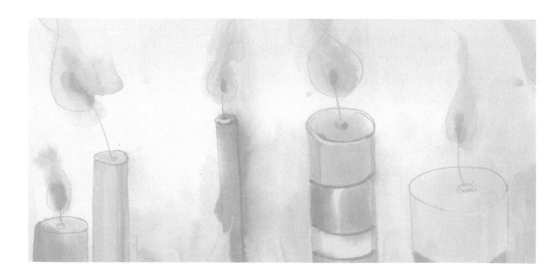

CHRISTMAS EVE, 1979

My son is 4 days old today. He and I are in University College Hospital, London. During the pregnancy I had dreaded being in hospital over Christmas, but now I'm loving it. The hospital has allowed the baby's father and other friends to be with me at any time, for as long as I want, so I haven't felt cut off, as I'd feared. In fact, because it is Christmas, everyone is off work and has more time to spend than usual; visiting me in hospital and celebrating has become the thing to do.

We have been celebrating with drink, chocolates and cigarettes since teatime. The Irish sister brought them round on a mortuary trolley earlier. The nurses have dressed up as fairies and are delivering presents to all the babies and mothers. Everyone is slightly high. I have been high on the birth of my son for days. He sleeps in a plastic tub on wheels and I can't take my eyes off him – I still can't believe he's real.

Out of the window, even the heart of London seems hushed and glowing, expectant for Christmas. I have never seen Tottenham Court Road without traffic before.

Diana Allsopp

THE NOW CAROL

(Tunes: Irby, Gott des Himmels (Albert), St Leonard or All Saints)

In the dark a woman, waiting,
Fills each pain with laboured breath,
Still unsure what lies before her.
Will the dawn bring life or death?
Mary's song still echoes clear:
Justice, hope, and peace are near.

By her side, a man sits quiet,
Knows he cannot share her pain.
Still he stays, all sleep refusing,
Prays, and holds, and prays again.
Mary's song still echoes clear:
Justice, hope, and peace are near.

Round this birth, as every other,
Wars are fought and people flee;
Each new mother feeds her baby
With a yearning to be free.
Mary's song still echoes clear:
Justice, hope, and peace are near.

Now, as Mary feels the crowning,
Still she wonders how this birth,
God's desire and her responding,
Holds the power to heal the earth.
Mary's song still echoes clear:
Justice, hope, and peace are near.

Joseph watches God emerging,
Tiny, frail, a breast to find;
Wonders how one woman's labour
Bears the key for humankind.
Mary's song still echoes clear:
Justice, hope, and peace are near.

Woman, Man, together finding
God has given each their worth,
In their answer to God's calling
Bring the Word of life to birth.
Mary's song still echoes clear:
Justice, hope, and peace are near.

Anna Briggs

YOU ARE DEEPLY, DEEPLY LOVED

On this night of the year, a voice is speaking – can we hear it?

'I know the cares and the anxious thoughts of your hearts.
I know the hard time you often give yourselves.
I know the hopes and ambitions that you have for yourselves and for others.
I know your doubts, too – even while you seek to express your belief.

On this night, I want to find a way of saying to you:

You are deeply, deeply loved,
just as you are,
forgiven, loved and challenged to be
the very best you can be.
So I'm speaking to you in the only way I know how –
from a stable,
in a child born into poverty,
soon to grow to maturity,
born to show you,
in a human life,
the love of God.'

John Harvey

COME, LIGHT OF LIFE

Lord,
in the beginning
when all was very dark, you said:
'Let there be light.'
And there was light
and life throughout the universe.

And when the human race
was exhausted, tired and weary,
in the darkness of anxiety,
confusion and sin,
into that darkness you came
as light in Jesus Christ.
God became a human being among us all.

Once again it is dark.
Not just dark at midnight
but dark in ourselves:
dark with doubt,
dark with fear and uncertainty,
dark with confusing
and conflicting voices in our ears.

Come, Light of life,
lighten the darkness in our lives
with your mighty word of love.
Lighten our hearts with the joy
of your promised coming.
Lighten our world with the hope
that faith in you still brings.

We go out into Christmas Day
in the peace of Jesus Christ.
May his peace,
that lightens the soul with faith,
lifts the spirit with hope
and leavens the world with love,
be yours tonight and always.

And the blessing of God,
the Creator, the Son and the Spirit,
go with you, and remain with you
now and always.
Amen

John Harvey

LEONARD

The weak ones of our society have taught me so much. They have shown me what it is to live simply, to love tenderly, to speak in truth, to pardon, to receive openly, to be humble in weakness, to be confident in difficulties and to accept handicaps and hardships with love.
Jean Vanier, L'Arche Community

Matthew 5:14–16; John 1:1–18

It didn't feel like Christmas Eve. I didn't even want to go to mass. I was so tired. So tired of all the hassles and arguments all day. Arguments between assistants and core members, assistants and assistants, core members and core members … The household was divided. It was three against two, two against three. Alfred had thrown himself on the floor, Rita had thrown and broken her cup, Pierrette had cried that Christmas was ruined – and closed her eyes and prayed to God that we'd all just go away, her face scrunched up tight like a fist. Like a discarded invitation, left lying in a ball in the corner.

It had been one long day of frustrated expectation. Like an endless trip to get some place special we never ever arrived at, and that kept receding in flatness. Everybody became twitchy and irritable. We'd been talking about Christmas coming for weeks. It was like we were all sitting waiting for the magic and love to open up and when it didn't we started blaming each other. We tried opening one gift each, to see if that would help – help open the magic and love a crack – but nothing happened. In everything we tried something was missing.

I just wanted to go to bed.

We piled into the van. Didn't speak on the way. Pierrette started to sing along to some radio jingle and Rita told her to shut up I got a headache. With her cleft palette it sounded like 'heartache'. 'I got a heartache.' We couldn't find a place to park, and so had to walk; piled out into the cold. Pierrette forgot her mittens. 'Why do you always forget your mittens, Pierrette?' 'She does it on purpose,' someone accused. Pierrette cried that she did not do it on purpose! Alfred muttered and swore under his breath – like he was full up with everything everyone was thinking and feeling all day and it had to come out. In a litany. The winter night clouded with curses.

We met Leonard inside the cathedral. Leonard lived in our house too and shared a room with Matt; he'd been away at a Christmas party for his workshop. He clapped and danced when he saw us (I couldn't understand why); stood wearing a paper hat and a dumb look that made Rita suddenly start laughing. 'Ha, look at Leonard,' she pointed, 'what a fool. You're a fool, Leonard,' she sang, carrying herself along in a huff, then resting. Leonard's workshop made little wooden boats and trains that the community shop sold. He went around shaking all our hands, like he had some good news to share; his grip, rooted and bracing, his breath, warm and sweet, smelling of Christmas cookies and shortbread, fruit cake seasoned with rum. We got all tangled together and touched. The big bell pealed and Leonard led us in through the heavy doors with a dance-walk. He looked brilliant in his party clothes.

We were late, and slow, and they started without us. We had to find some space in back; God seemed far away. The cathedral domed and towered, and we gazed up at the rich, golden light every place. 'Wow,' said Rita. There were families and couples everywhere, fancy women, children dressed in their nicest clothes, best behaviour. There was a choir of boys somewhere; distant, faint drafts of spicy, sweet incense.

Pierrette closed her eyes when you were supposed to, opened them when you were supposed to, but nothing happened. Her face remained worried. Alfred had to go to the washroom, and Gus, my colleague, took him. Matt kept biting the skin around his fingernails. When it came time for communion at last, Leonard was the only one who stood at the invitation. Rita said: 'No, yeah, you go for us, Leonard,' and slid down in the pew. I said I'd take him, and Leonard led me up the long road of red carpet.

When we reached the crossing, he stopped by a deserted side chapel and turned and signed to me – signed to me to come, come follow, and ducked inside. The chapel was warm and embracing; stone walls flickered and glowed. I sat down in a window recess to wait. We'd be home soon, I thought and glanced at my watch.

Leonard stood in front of a crucifix and crossed himself. It was never easy to understand Leonard when he spoke with words; you had to really listen, know him (Christ understood perfectly). Leonard prayed aloud and in the rise and fall of language I recognised the name of his friend Charlie who had died two Christmases ago. Charlie had Down's, and had lived in the same institution as Leonard before coming to live in community. Charlie and Leonard were like brothers, and the loss made Leonard sad and heavy at times – so that he wouldn't come dance in the living room when you put the Bay City Rollers record on; wouldn't change his dirty clothes when you told him to and turned up your tone.

Leonard prayed for the soul of his friend – his name whispered in the chapel and settled in the arms of Christ, gently, lovingly. I closed my eyes; and in the peace prayed to Jesus to take away the sadness and weight I still wore like dirty clothes. I could feel myself begin to settle down into a more rooted place. I became aware of my breathing. My crowded, busy mind. After a moment, Leonard tapped me on the shoulder – took my hand.

When we made it to the front finally, Leonard solemnly stepped forward – then suddenly stole the chalice out of the priest's hands and – with his strong thirst, profound spirit – drank the wine down in a few quick gulps. Like he wanted to drink deep the drafts of God alive. Like he'd been sitting in the middle of a desert and it was an emergency, and he had to drink enough for the whole of us.

'Aaaaaaah,' he said, and licked his lips. Wore a purple ring.

I started to open in a smile. The priest didn't smile, and carefully, seriously took the cup back (never exactly let go). He signed something in Latin (Christ understood perfectly). I seized the bread and wine of the moment, and Leonard and I walked around the cathedral with our tapers, lit up now. 'Wow, wow,' he kept saying – the eternal 'wow' – gazing around at all the points of light, at all the people: like stars coming out; his boyish face lit up with a zing, like when you helped him shave and he slapped on Skin Bracer. He stopped and gazed up at his Mother Mary with a such a deep, human love that light spilled from his eyes. She held her arms out to the whole world, and Leonard wanted to reach out and hug everybody in the congregation. And some responded warmly, and shook his hand, and others remained seated inside themselves; couldn't, wouldn't flow out to him; stared past him like he wasn't there; smiled politely, faces shining with a clean, hard light – like polished brass, like a gold pendant; kept their hearts cordoned. Some treated him like a child and preciously. Others gave him looks that said it was not how they believed people should behave inside this institution. Some glanced away, embarrassed by all his dancing openness, naked feeling showing. And others looked as if they wished they could embrace him, break free. As we passed through the crowd and I recognised my frightened selves reflected back. I caught up to Leonard; took his hand.

Leonard loved the children and the little babies, all bundled up. I assured one young mother that it was all right, that he was very gentle, and she let him put his face up and say hallo; he beamed like the sun. The tired woman looked into Leonard's warm, beaming face and handed him her child to hold and rock a minute. Leonard kissed the baby's forehead, left a mark of glistening. The baby stopped crying, and the woman smiled a moment; looked less pursued in that light – more a hopeful follower of the future than a sad-eyed refugee from a past.

I handed Leonard back his candle; and he turned and carried it to where the others were left sitting; walked with slow ceremony down the long aisle, shielding and cradling the fragile warm flame that trembled and bounced. The priest was declaiming that God was the Light that the darkness could never extinguish, and that Christ was the Light of the world; that we were all light and loved and held in God's hand; and as he was speaking, Leonard passed the light from the tip of his taper down the dark line of us … Pierrette gazed down with wonder at the light she was holding and swallowed – then suddenly smiled. Rita looked at her light and laughed – a nervous flicker at first, then out loud, held high. Matt looked at his light, his dark eyes glowing with shy halos inside. Alfred looked at his, and was silent. One by one our faces lit up; with each new light all our separate lights seemed to grow stronger, more confident; there was a warm feeling passed down through us; down the line like forgiveness. I turned to Gus and we looked one another in the eye; shook hands: acknowledging the light in each other. Leonard and Matt embraced. Everyone in the cathedral stood to sing the final hymn, Hark the Herald Angels Sing; held hands; candles aloft. Rita knew all of the words. Didn't need to look at the book like other people did. Gus teased her that she looked like the Statue of Liberty and Rita told him to shut up she was singing; gave him a good slap. He called her it again. Pierrette said she never wanted the moment to end, and closed her eyes down upon it tightly. The bell rang out for Christmas Day and you could feel it shiver all through you.

The priest gave the final blessing, and, free of heavy shadow, we were vaulted up into the heavenly music, warm feeling. Families and neighbours were all kissing and hugging. 'Wow. Wow,' Leonard kept saying, like he kept seeing shooting stars every place. Suddenly all the lights in the cathedral were switched on from somewhere: like an explosion from a long lit fuse. Down inside I felt the warm, still centre Leonard had led me back to. Like a perpetual light set there.

Leonard went around saluting the priest and altar boys, clapping his hands, drunk on Holy Spirit. Matt copied him. Then found his own style, dance. 'Hey, look at Matt,' cried Rita. 'what a clown. You're a clown, Matt.'

We walked out together, holding hands like one big family. Rita walked with an angel in her step, like her legs weren't bothering her at all any more.

I'd gone into church depressed and exhausted and had emerged with a starry feeling and the energy of love.

'Look it, snow!' cried Pierrette. And suddenly everyone held out their hands; started catching it on their tongues. Strangers. Neighbours we didn't know – big, soft, floaty flakes that hung on to our coats and mittens and eyelashes. It was like the hand of heaven had opened up. There was a life-sized nativity scene on the front lawn, all lit up. The night was like a million lit tapers and I stopped to breathe in the wonder a moment: the light, rich, heady scent of snow, like bread rising, before we hopped in the van and sang Gloria all the way home. Rita said her headache was gone. 'I'm a good singer,' she told us. 'You're a good singer, Pierrette,' she told Pierrette.

We stayed up late and drank the wine we didn't all have in church. Leonard didn't drink and had Pepsi Cola. The living room was warm and homey and we switched off the lights a moment to see the tree all lit up. 'Wow!' we all cried at once, and sat wrapped in silence, it was so beautiful. Pierrette said it was beautiful the way everyone all helped to decorate the tree. 'I can see where Rita helped, and I can see where Alfred helped, and I can see where Matthew helped …' Red wine glanced and shimmered in my mug; I could smell the cinnamon and cloves, and evergreen. We switched the lights back on and tried to guess our Chris Kinders. Matt and Leonard played Santa. Leonard got jumbo bubble bath. Gus said, 'Great, now we'll never get him outta the tub!' Matt got more Legos. Pierrette got slippers and a cookbook to try. Alfred got new clothes his family sent him. Rita got a new mug that played Jingle Bells. Gus got a funny T-shirt; I got a serious book. Pierrette said we all had gifts, and closed her eyes and prayed for peace and joy for all God's people this holy night – her beautiful face relaxed and peaceful and open, like it could hold the whole world.

Prayer

Jesus, I think of you as someone
who'd clap and dance and
be happy to see his friends.

Who'd move with a dance in his walk
and open heavy doors.

Who'd wear a party hat and play the fool.

Who'd be unafraid to show love,
who'd reach across and hug everyone.

Who'd grab away the cup and offend the priests.
Who'd be looked upon as simple.

Who'd bring light to the deserted and
help open up the night.
Who'd help open gifts.

Who'd see shooting stars every place
and chant 'Wow!'

Jesus, help me to recognise you
in unexpected people and places.
Amen

Neil Paynter

BIDDING PRAYERS FOR CHRISTMAS EVE

Bright Holy God,
You come among us.
You fill us with awe and wonder.
You welcome our stories and our prayers …

We pray tonight for peace, peace in places where there is anger and war and fear … We pray for peacemakers and peacekeepers, for rulers, for politicians, for fighters, for older people and children … for all who are caught up in conflict, in bitterness and in danger … We pray for peace with integrity and with justice.

God, in your mercy,
HEAR OUR PRAYER.

We pray on this night for travellers … for those who are travelling home for Christmas … for those who are travelling because they have no place, no shelter they can call their own … for those whose home is on the road.

God, in your mercy,
HEAR OUR PRAYER.

We pray for the children who will be born tonight and for their families.
We ask your blessing on their lives …

God, in your mercy,
HEAR OUR PRAYER.

We pray for all who are sick, and for those who care for them and pray for them …

We pray for those who have died, for those we miss at our table … tell them how much we love them … and miss them … tell them we carry their stories in our lives.

God, in your mercy,
HEAR OUR PRAYER.

We pray for ourselves, for our needs, for our worries, for our hopes and dreams …

God, in your mercy,
HEAR OUR PRAYER.

Emmanuel, God with us,

heaven come down to earth,
help us tonight to listen to the angels
and not be afraid of you,
of your weakness or your glory.
Come, Holy helpless Jesus.
Come into our lives with joy. AMEN

Ruth Burgess

CHRISTMAS EVE INVOCATION

Burst into the world
as a wrinkled and bloodied newborn child,
and shock us with your vulnerability
and your crying need.

Come into the world
as one of the insignificant ones
for whom the world can find no room.
Confront us with the squalor of the animal shed
where Mary laboured for you,
cried out for you, shed her blood for you,
went to death's gates to push you into life.

Come into the world
as a child on the edge,
granted safe space
by a man not your father.

Come to us in your defencelessness,
your mother's agony for you,
your foster-father's acceptance of you.

Come to us
as we wait.

Maranatha

Amen

Annie Heppenstall-West

WE'VE MUCKED OUT THE STABLE

We've mucked out
the stable
and put down the
plush carpet;

still,
you will come:
tracking in mud
from the Jordan
and shaking sin's dust
off your clothes.

The animals have
been dropped off at the SPCA,
and the room deodorised;

still,
you will come:
leading the lost,
the least, the little
into our midst.

We've turned over the manger
and covered it with Irish lace,
setting the table
with the finest silver and china;

still,
you will come:
tearing the linen into strips
for binding our wounds,
selling the silver
to feed the hungry.

We've tamed
and made marketable
this most holy of nights,
shaping it by our own desires and dilemmas;

still,
you will come:

slipping between
the cracks in our despair
to fill our emptiness with grace
and the carols of angels;
to transform our acquisitiveness
into generosity.

Thom M Shuman

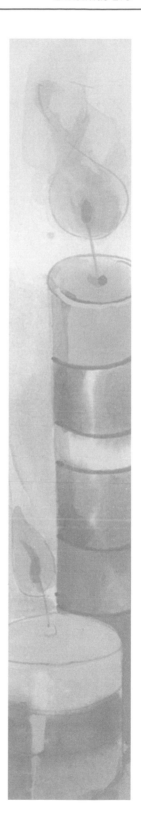

ROCK US GENTLY

Rock us
Rock us gently
ROCK US WITH LOVE

Cradle us
Cradle us tenderly
CRADLE US WITH LOVE

Swaddle us
Swaddle us firmly
SWADDLE US WITH LOVE

Bless us
Bless us kindly
BLESS US WITH LOVE.

Ruth Burgess

TONIGHT

Tonight we are excited
BLESS US WITH WONDER

Tonight we are expectant
BLESS US WITH GLADNESS

Tonight we are on tiptoe
BLESS US WITH NEW BIRTH

Ruth Burgess

IT'S NEARLY CHRISTMAS

Tonight
I am excited.

It's nearly Christmas.

Tonight
the stars
are shining brightly.

Tonight
it's hard
to go to sleep,

but I'm trying.

Thank you
for my
warm bed.

Tomorrow
will be happy.

I'll get presents.

Tomorrow
You will smile
at me.

Happy
Birthday
baby Jesus.

Ruth Burgess

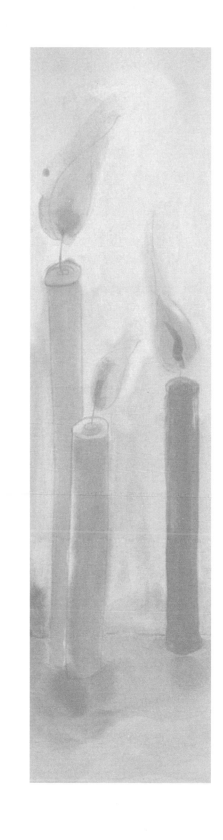

SOURCES AND ACKNOWLEDGEMENTS

Every effort has been made to trace copyright holders of all the items reproduced in this book. We would be glad to hear from anyone whom we have been unable to contact so that any omissions can be rectified in future editions.

Pg.16   'Beinn A' Chochuill' was first published in the *Epworth Review*.

Pg.17   'I'm not going to sing' was first published in *At Ground Level*, Ruth Burgess, Wild Goose Publications (out of print).

Pg.24   'The saints of God' – Words and music by Ian M Fraser. © 2004 Stainer & Bell Ltd. Used by permission of Stainer & Bell.

Pg.31   Quote from Margery Kempe from *The Mirror of Love: Daily readings with Marjory Kempe*, edited by Gillian Hawker, Darton, Longman & Todd, ISBN 0 232517 83 5

Pg.32   Quote from Julian of Norwich from *Enfolded in Love: Daily readings with Julian of Norwich*, Darton, Longman & Todd, ISBN 0 232514 85 2. Used by permission of Darton, Longman & Todd

Pg.33   'Pentecost' – Words by Ian M Fraser © 2001 Stainer & Bell Ltd. Used by permission of Stainer & Bell.

Pg.34   'November' was first published in *At Ground Level,* Ruth Burgess, Wild Goose Publications (out of print).

Pg.40   'St Martin of Tours' – Music by John Barnard, words by Kathy Galloway. Music © John Barnard/Jubilate Hymns. Used by permission of John Barnard/Jubilate Hymns and Hope Publishing Company. Words used by permission of Kathy Galloway.

Pg.55   'The people God calls blessed' was first published in *A Book of Blessings*, Ruth Burgess, Wild Goose Publications, 2001, ISBN 1901557480.

Pg.101   'Come and light the candles' (Advent candle song) was first published in *Christian Aid – Life Before Death, 1993 Advent material*. © Janet Morley and Christian Aid. Used by permission Janet Morley and Christian Aid.

Pg.134   'Sheep' was first printed in *The Coracle*, the magazine of the Iona Community, April 1999. ionacomm@gla.iona.org.uk

Pg.134   'I walk dangerous paths' was first published in *Pushing The Boat Out*, edited by Kathy Galloway, Wild Goose Publications, 1995. ISBN 0947988742.

Pg.144   'My mother was not most pleased' was first published in the *Epworth Review*.

Pg.145   'Victory' was first published in *Coracle*, the magazine of the Iona Community, May 1994. ionacomm@gla.iona.org.uk

Pg.146   'Death is a lonely place' was first published in *Pushing The Boat Out*, edited by Kathy Galloway, Wild Goose Publications, 1995. ISBN 0947988742.

Pg.147   'Waiting' was first published in *Coracle*, the magazine of the Iona Community, December 2002. ionacomm@gla.iona.org.uk

Pg.148   'Over' was first published in *At Ground Level*, Ruth Burgess, Wild Goose Publications (out of print).

Pg.162   Richard Horsley quote from 'Who is your Saviour?', *The Other Side* magazine, Nov/Dec 2003, p.22. Originally from *Christmas Unwrapped Consumerism, Christ and Culture*, edited by Richard Horsley and James Tracy, Trinity Press International in 2001. Quote used by permission of Richard Horsley.

Pg.166   'God, wake us up' © Jan Berry. From *Gateways of Grace*, the Prayer Handbook 1998–99. Published by the United Reformed Church.

Pg.178   'Stars' was first published in *At Ground Level*, Ruth Burgess, Wild Goose Publications (out of print).

Pg.200   'Come, God' © Ruth Burgess. First published in *Bread of Tomorrow: Praying with the world's poor*, Janet Morley, SPCK, 1992. ISBN 0281056986

Pg.208   'Good enough' was first published in *From Imaginary Conversations: Dialogues for use in worship and Bible study*, Jan Sutch Pickard, Methodist Church Overseas Division, 1989/90.

Pg.214   'Choosing God' © Ruth Burgess. First published in *Bread of Tomorrow: Praying with the world's poor*, Janet Morley, SPCK, 1992. ISBN 0281056986

Pg.221   'O round as the world is the orange you give us! (Carol for a Christingle service)', by Fred Pratt Green. © 1979 Stainer & Bell Ltd. Used by permission of Stainer & Bell and Hope Publishing Company.

Pg.230   'Advent hymn', by Jan Berry, first published in *Encircling Prayer 2*, The Partnership for Theological Education, Manchester 2003. Used with permission of Jan Berry.

Pg.234   'Christmas prayer' by Carol Dixon, from a Christmas pack published by John Paul The Preacher's Press, 1991 (out of print). Used by permission of Carol Dixon and John Paul The Preacher's Press.

INDEX OF AUTHORS

ABOUT THE CONTRIBUTORS

Unfortunately it was not possible to obtain biographical details of all the contributors.

Alison Adam is a member of the Iona Community.

Diana Allsopp is 'originally Christian but now a Quaker attender and Taoist'.

Enid Ayers is a member of Janus Writers in Sunderland and Christian Writers Group in Durham.

Irene Barratt was born in 1934 in Oldham. She taught adults with learning difficulties until retirement in 2000, and then studied to be a Methodist local preacher. She is married with two children and two grandsons.

Jan Berry is a minister in the United Reformed Church and a tutor in Practical Theology at Northern College, Manchester (part of the Partnership for Theological Education). She enjoys writing and creating liturgy, and is currently working on a Ph.D on women's rituals of transition.

Cally Booker lives in Dundee where she contributes to the liturgy at St Paul's Cathedral.

Anna Briggs – an artist, writer, singer, knitter and clown, born on Tyneside, lived all over, always looking for something new to make and reach people with, especially people who are out of the loop of love and meaning through illness, war, poverty or some other label or event.

Alix Brown is a therapist working mainly with traumatised adolescents. She is a member of the Iona Community and lives in Shropshire with her partner, Polly, and a selection of animals.

Ruth Burgess is a writer and an editor who lives in the North East of England with a large and hungry black and white cat. She enjoys markets and fireworks and growing flowers and food. She is a member of the Iona Community.

David J.M. Coleman is a member of the Iona Community and a minister at Barrhead Church Covenant, near Glasgow. He is married to Zam Walker and is a parent to Taliesin and Melangell. He is inspired by the subversive ecumenical potential of orthodox Christianity, and looks forward to the challenge to the closed canon of 'official' hymnbooks as the churches embrace electronic media, which are already vital to his day-to-day grassroots ministry.

Frances Copsey – 'I continue to struggle with words and MS, and now with the internet too!' More poems by Frances Copsey at www.msplus.pwp.blueyonder.co.uk

Ian Cowie came to the Iona Community on leaving the hospital and army back in 1945. He was the first Iona Abbey guide, then served as a minister in three parishes and finally as chaplain to the Christian Fellowship of Healing. He published five books: *Growing Knowing Jesus, People Praying, Across the Spectrum, Prayer and Ideas for Healing Services* (Wild Goose Publications), and *Jesus' Healing Works and Ours* (Wild Goose Publications), and was a regular contributor to Wild Goose anthologies. Ian died in 2005 at age 81..

Katrina Crosby is a former member of the Iona Community's resident group on Iona.

James Curry is a member of the Iona Community and an Anglican priest in Jarrow. He enjoys folk music, real ale and malt whisky, and holidays in Scotland and Northumberland.

John Davies is a member of the Iona Community and a parish priest. He writes online at www.johndavies.org

Carol Dixon was born and brought up in Alnwick, Northumberland and is a lay preacher in the United Reformed Church, recently serving as the National Lay Preaching Commissioner. She works as Moderator's secretary in the Northern Synod Office, is a member of an ecumenical prayer fellowship, the Companions of Brother Lawrence, and is a Friend of St Cuthbert's, Holy Island. She enjoys writing Northumbrian songs, and her hymns have been published in *All Year Round, Songs for the New Millennium, Worship Live* and the new Church of Scotland hymnary. She is married and has a daughter and twin sons.

David Fox was born in Newbridge, Monmouthshire. He studied chemistry at University College London and taught for a while in Reading. Now a minister of the United Reformed Church serving in Penarth, he has contributed to a number of ecumenical publications for Cytûn and CTBI.

Ian M Fraser – 'The main thing about my life is that Margaret married me, I have three children, nine grandchildren and two great-grandchildren. I became a member of the Iona Community in 1941.'

Kathy Galloway is the current leader of the Iona Community.

Ray Gaston is a priest at All Hallows Church in Hyde Park, an inner city area of Leeds, England.

Liz Gibson lives in Oban with her husband Martyn and their sons Paul and Hamish. She is a Church of Scotland minister and a hospital chaplain. She brings her experience of theatre and literature to her church's Worship Group. Becoming a member of the Iona Community in1998, she has been involved with the community's centres on Iona and at Camas on the Isle of Mull.

David Hamflett is a Methodist minister and a friend of the Iona Community, working in the north of England. He has a special interest in compiling and composing liturgies. He also particularly enjoys playing and singing traditional folk songs and tunes.

John Harvey is a member of the Iona Community.

Margaret Harvey is a founder member of Coleg y Groes Community and helps to run Coleg y Groes Retreat House in Corwen, North Wales (www.colegygroes.co.uk). She is a native of Wales and a Church of Wales priest.

Pam Hathorn has been a senior special needs teacher in Berkshire for many years. She is looking forward to a new lease of life and new directions as she leaves teaching behind.

Annie Heppenstall-West was born in Yorkshire, grew up in the Midlands, studied theology at Cambridge, then came back to Yorkshire, where she lives with her husband and son. She is a member of All Hallows Church, Leeds.

Alan Horner was Chairman of the Methodist Synod in Scotland 1982–84. He retired from paid ministry in 1999 and moved to Milton Keynes to work for the Living Spirituality Network as Associate staff.

Judith Jessop is a Methodist minister currently working in Sheffield and a single parent caring for her two children. She has been a Fairtrader for many years, would like to pursue issues of justice and peace, and is interested in new ways of thinking about and shaping Christian faith. She enjoys theatre and cinema.

Beryl Jeanne is an artist, wordsmith, creative retreat leader and mother, who lives and worships in Birmingham.

Pat Livingstone splits her time between composing, teaching and playing music. In 2005 she worked as Head of Lewisham Music Service overseeing the provision of instrumental/vocal/curriculum music teaching in the borough. She is always thinking about composing and occasionally gets time to do it! The full score of 'Winter Lights' is available from the composer at info@oranmusic.org.uk .

Rachel Mann is an Anglican curate in South Manchester. As a poet and liturgist she aims to enable people to encounter the gaps between words where God waits to make herself known. Her perfect day involves watching creaky old films, eating good food and drinking even better wine.

Mary McHugh lives in Durham and works as a doctor at Sunderland Royal Hospital. For the last two years she has been President of the National Board of Catholic Women.

Kate McIlhagga was a minister, latterly in Northumberland, involved in writing, retreat work and the local hospice until she died in 2002. She was a member of the Iona Community.

Peter Millar is a member of the Iona Community and author of several books, including *Our Hearts Still Sing* (Wild Goose Publications).

Yvonne Morland is a member of the Iona Community.

Rosie Morton – Currently curate at All Saints Church, King's Heath, Birmingham, Rosie enjoys time with friends and family, travelling, creative writing and being outdoors, preferably climbing mountains. She was a contributor to Ruth Burgess' book *Friends and Enemies*, Wild Goose Publications.

Carolyn Morris was a teacher in primary schools and in hospitals for many years. She is now appreciating life in a new way as an author-craftsperson.

Debra Mullaly is a member of a large family living in Durham. She attends a comprehensive school where she is recognised for her caring attitude to other children, especially those with difficulties.

Jean Murdoch died in spring 2003. She lived in Oban and was an associate member of the Iona Community.

Liz Paterson worked with the Church of Uganda, doing community development for 16 years. During this time, she was involved with AIDS and HIV education, including working for 3 years with an orphan support organisation. AIDS has affected many of her friends and colleagues. She has been a member of the Iona Community since 1986.

Neil Paynter has worked in nursing homes, homeless shelters and homes for people with various challenges. He is now an editor/writer. His books include *Lent & Easter Readings from Iona, This is the Day: Readings and Meditations from the Iona Community, Blessed Be Our Table,* and *Holy Ground* (with Helen Boothroyd), all published by Wild Goose.

Jan Sutch Pickard is a poet and storyteller, Methodist lay preacher and a member of the Iona Community, based in Mull. For six years she worked on Iona, latterly as Warden of the Abbey. As this publication went to press, she was volunteering on the West Bank with the Ecumenical Accompaniment Programme of the World Council of Churches.

Chris Polhill is a member of the Iona Community and co-author of *Eggs & Ashes: Liturgical and Practical Resources for Lent and Easter* (Wild Goose Publications).

Gary Polhill is a scientist and lives in Aberdeen.

Thom M Shuman is a poet and Presbyterian pastor in Cincinnati, Ohio, where he lives with his wife, Bonnie. His son, Teddy, a cancer survivor as well as a person with multiple disabilities, lives nearby. Thom blogs at www.occasionalsighting.blogspot.com

Josie Smith has been a teacher, a freelance radio and TV broadcaster, a Methodist preacher, and worked for 13 years on the staff of the Methodist headquarters. She is now actively retired in Sheffield.

Liz Gregory-Smith lives with her husband in Durham and has two adult sons. Since retiring from teaching, she has been a reader in her village church, St. Catherine's. She is also involved in a creative writing project with day guests at St Cuthbert's Hospice in Durham.

Nancy Somerville is a widely published poet and a member of Edinburgh's Shore Poets. www.shorepoets.org.uk She is a Community Education worker and an associate of the Iona Community.

Patricia Stoat was born in London, and has lived in Tyneside and Japan; she is now living in Nottingham, where she is involved with refugees and asylum seekers, and with developing community prison chaplaincy. She is a lifelong feminist who sees no conflict between feminism and the Christian faith.

Marjorie Tolchard – 'I am a retired school librarian. I have two stepsons and a son and a daughter, all grown up and flown the nest. One of my stepsons has a 13-year-old son. The other has a 10-year-old son and a 3-year-old daughter. I live in a very small village in Northamptonshire where I edit the village newsletter and write a local news column for the local weekly paper. My hobbies are gardening, writing and embroidery. I belong to a local history society, a gardening club and two writers' groups.

Elizabeth Varley is a parish priest in North Yorkshire and an associate member of the Iona Community.

Rosie Watson is a wife, mother, grandmother and a former special needs teacher, working latterly with young offenders. She cannot remember a time when Jesus was not her friend, though for years he hid his face. She lives in Hertfordshire with her husband.

Davie Webster worked as a maintenance man on Iona with the Iona Community and with the Cathedral Trustees. He died in 1994.

Wellspring was born in 1998 when Catherine McElhinney and Kathryn Turner began making resources, used in parishes and schools, available to the wider world, particularly through their website www.wellsprings.org.uk

Brian Woodcock is a former warden of Iona Abbey and a URC minister in St Alban's.

THE IONA COMMUNITY IS:

- An ecumenical movement of men and women from different walks of life and different traditions in the Christian church
- Committed to the gospel of Jesus Christ, and to following where that leads, even into the unknown
- Engaged together, and with people of goodwill across the world, in acting, reflecting and praying for justice, peace and the integrity of creation
- Convinced that the inclusive community we seek must be embodied in the community we practise

Together with our staff, we are responsible for:

- Our islands residential centres of Iona Abbey, the MacLeod Centre on Iona, and Camas Adventure Centre on the Ross of Mull

and in Glasgow:

- The administration of the Community
- Our work with young people
- Our publishing house, Wild Goose Publications
- Our association in the revitalising of worship with the Wild Goose Resource Group

The Iona Community was founded in Glasgow in 1938 by George MacLeod, minister, visionary and prophetic witness for peace, in the context of the poverty and despair of the Depression. Its original task of rebuilding the monastic ruins of Iona Abbey became a sign of hopeful rebuilding of community in Scotland and beyond. Today, we are about 250 Members, mostly in Britain, and 1500 Associate Members, with 1400 Friends worldwide. Together and apart, 'we follow the light we have, and pray for more light'.

For information on the Iona Community contact:
The Iona Community, Fourth Floor, Savoy House, 140 Sauchiehall Street,
Glasgow G2 3DH, UK. Phone: 0141 332 6343
e-mail: ionacomm@gla.iona.org.uk; web: www.iona.org.uk

For enquiries about visiting Iona, please contact:
Iona Abbey, Isle of Iona, Argyll PA76 6SN, UK. Phone: 01681 700404
e-mail: ionacomm@iona.org.uk

ALSO FROM WILD GOOSE PUBLICATIONS ...

MORE RESOURCES FOR ADVENT & CHRISTMAS:

Hay & Stardust
Resources for Christmas to Candlemas
Ruth Burgess

This companion resource book to *Candles & Conifers* covers the season of Christmastide, including Christmas Eve, Holy Innocents' Day, Winter and New Year, Epiphany, Homelessness Sunday and Candlemas. It also contains eight Christmas plays, including a puppet play.

ISBN 1 905010 00 1

Hear My Cry
A daily prayer book for Advent
Ruth Burgess

A daily prayer book for Advent which can also be used as a prayer journal, taking its inspiration from the Advent antiphons – a group of prayers that reflect on the character and activities of God. The format for each day includes a Bible verse, an Advent cry and suggestions for prayer. The pages can be added to and personalised, with line drawings that can be coloured in and space to add your own pictures, reflections and prayers. Instructions for three workshops are also included to enable Advent themes to be explored in a group setting.

ISBN 1 901557 95 2

The Jesse Tree
Thom Shuman

We know the familiar stories like Noah and the Ark; we know the famous people, like Mary and David – but what about those people who might only be mentioned once in the Bible (in the lineages in Matthew and Luke)? What about those folks that Jesus might have heard about at bedtime? What about the women, the prophets, the exiles who, while not linked to Jesus genetically, nevertheless passed on their 'spiritual DNA' to him and to us? They are just as much a part of his heritage, his family, his 'tree' as all his relatives by blood and by marriage. They are a part of the tradition and faith we seek to pass onto our children and grandchildren. They are branches on the Jesse tree.

ISBN 1 905010 06 0

Cloth for the Cradle
Worship resources & readings for Advent, Christmas and Epiphany
Wild Goose Worship Group

This rediscovery of the stories of Christ's birth through adult eyes contains much to reflect on individually and to use in group and worship situations. The material is drawn from the work of the Wild Goose Resource and Worship Groups whose innovative style of worship is widely admired and imitated.

SBN 1 901557 01 4

Innkeepers and Light Sleepers
Seventeen new songs for Christmas   Songbook/CD
John L Bell

My bonnie boy • He became poor • Christmas is coming • Carol of the Advent • No wind at the window • Justice in the womb • And did it happen • Look up and wonder • God immersed in mystery • Funny kind of night • The pedigree • Ma wee bit dearie • Ho ro ho ro • The aye carol • Simeon's song • Carol of the Epiphany • The refugees

Songbook ISBN 0 947988 47 5
Cassette ISBN 0 947988 54 8
CD ISBN 1 901557 39 1

Advent Readings from Iona
Brian Woodcock & Jan Sutch Pickard

Celebrate Christmas with reflections and prayers for each day of Advent. This effective antidote to the commercialism of the festive season can be used for individual meditation or group worship. The authors are the former wardens of the Abbey on the Isle of Iona.

ISBN 1 905010 33 2

ALSO FROM WILD GOOSE PUBLICATIONS ...

MORE BOOKS BY RUTH BURGESS:

Friends and Enemies
A book of short prayers & some ways to write your own
Ruth Burgess

A collection of prayers about relationships and the particular moments and places of our daily lives. They convey wisdom and humour, while some contain strong thoughts and words. 'Saying what we mean to God,' writes Ruth Burgess, 'is more honest than tiptoeing around the issues and concerns we find disturbing or difficult. To write with integrity is to write within the traditions of the writers of the psalms.' *Friends and Enemies* is offered as a resource for personal prayer and public worship, and as an encouragement to both individuals and congregations to be creative and courageous in their prayers. Includes three prayer-writing workshops.

ISBN 1 901557 78 2

Eggs & Ashes
Practical and liturgical resources for Lent and Holy Week
Ruth Burgess & Chris Polhill

Suitable for group worship or personal reflection, and with material for Shrove Tuesday, Ash Wednesday, Mothering Sunday, Palm Sunday and Holy Week, this is a collection to accompany readers through Lent and Easter for many years. Includes a Lent discipline for those who care about the environment, liturgies, responses, prayers, poems, reflections, meditations, stories, stations of the cross, sermons, monologues and songs, with some all-age resources – written by Iona Community members, associates, friends and others.

ISBN 1 901557 87 1

WWW.IONABOOKS.COM

Praying for the Dawn
A resource book for the ministry of healing
Ruth Burgess & Kathy Galloway

A compilation of material from several writers with strong emphasis on liturgies and resources for healing services. Includes a section on how to introduce healing services to those who may not be familiar with them, and suggestions for starting group discussions about healing. The book is rounded off by a section of worship resources – prayers, responses, litanies, poems, meditations and blessings.

ISBN 1 901557 26 X